"Massey-Harris 101"

A Letter to Generations X, Y, and Z: Quotations for the Ages

Curtis Dahlgren

AuthorHouse™
1663 Liberty Drive, Suite 200
Bloomington, IN 47403
www.authorhouse.com
Phone: 1-800-839-8640

© 2008 Curtis Dahlgren. All rights reserved.

No part of this book may be reproduced, stored in a retrieval system, or transmitted by any means without the written permission of the author.

First published by AuthorHouse   8/28/2008

ISBN: 978-1-4343-8777-6 (sc)

Library of Congress Control Number: 2008905158

Printed in the United States of America
Bloomington, Indiana

This book is printed on acid-free paper.

To Gramma Greenberg, Grampa Dahlgren,
and a few good friends.

"I wonder whether what we are publishing now is worth cutting down trees to make paper for the stuff."
- Richard Brautigan

"Of all the teachers I have known, I've found none greater than trees… Reach down as well as up. No roots, no branches."
- Douglas Wood
("Things Trees Know"; Adventure)

"I have learned a lot from trees; sometimes about the weather, sometimes about animals, sometimes about the Great Spirit."
- Walking Buffalo

"He who loves trees leaves mankind a little richer for his having lived."
- Martin L. Davey

"Read the best books first, or you may not be able to read them at all."
- Henry David Thoreau (1817-1862)

"These trees shall be my books."
- William Shakespeare

"The Tree of Life…"
- Moses

- Preface -

"At twenty years of age, the will reigns; at thirty, the wit; and at forty, the judgment."

- Benjamin Franklin (1706-1790)

"It will come as no surprise to anyone who has listened to a commencement speech in the last ten years to know that a spirit of elitism has been fostered among students - and deliberately - by politicians... Not so well known is the fact that many professors pander this same line to their classes... telling them how smart, how well educated they are...

"The words of politician and professor combine to reinforce the usual late-teenage ignorance; students of this age already assert their self-superiority. In short, too many professors pander to their audience and help the student to believe what his feelings of inadequacy have led him to assert: that he is smart and educated, that youth equates with eternal wisdom, that age equates with obstinacy and wrongness, and that the past has no lessons for the present.

"This attitude of elitism on the part of students is dangerous, for it quickly breeds a belief in their irresponsibility. They feel no obligation to family or society or country; in their quest for identity they place self above all those things that history has taught to be important.

"They feel themselves above everything. Thus they believe they are justified in using violence to enforce pacifism; they can shout down speakers with viewpoints in opposition to their own; they can throw beer bottles and trash out car windows while preaching against pollution.

"In short, their attitude of elitism leads them to believe they know better what is best for the country than do older or less educated yokels, and they intend to give it to the country whether it wants their solutions or not."

-"Professor X"
("This Beats Working For a Living";
Arlington House, 1973)

John Stuart Mill wrote about "the tyranny of prevailing opinion," but the "prevailing" opinions have become inverted 180 degrees from those of the culture in which he lived, and the tyranny of the Left in Academia is the deadliest of all. The worst "monopoly" in the world is Higher Education's monopoly of Thought.

Be wise with speed;
A fool at forty is a fool indeed.

- Andrew Young (1683-1765)

Table of Contents

Prologue   "Massey-Harris 101"........................7
Introduction to the Introduction
                "A letter to Generation XYZ".................25
Introduction   "Thinking outside the boxer shorts"............31
Chapter 1   The Traditional family vs. "Popular" culture......75
Chapter 2   Town vs. Gown: Traditional education
                vs. Politically correct "Higher" education.......119
Chapter 3   The New Media
                vs. the "Mainstream" news media.............157
Chapter 4   The People of the United States
                vs. the "Supreme" Court[s] 179
Epilogue   "Take heed that no man deceive you.".........229
Addendum   Back to School: DESSERTS can save your life...245

- Prologue -

"You ain't see no trouble yit."
                                    - Joel Chandler Harris

"This book is guaranteed to irritate nearly everybody... No wonder they poisoned Socrates; it was the only way they could get him to shut up."
                                    - Sydney J. Harris
                                    (on a book by Milton Mayer)

NEVER MIND FOR THE MOMENT WHY MY OPINIONS ARE SO OPINIONATED, but we need to talk! Today is George Washington's birthday (in "Black History" month, 2008) and on the eve of the eve of his birthday, the moon turned to red. In case you didn't notice during the eclipse, the two bright stars around the moon, plus the moon, created what almost looked like a clock in the sky. The big hand was on the 8 and the little hand just about on the 12. For Gen XYZ, that's 11:40; for us "old-timers," that's 20-to-12. Here's your sign: it's High Noon at the OK corral, or 12 PM on the old Atomic Clock. The party's over, almost, for Cinderella.

It was that fatal and perfidious bark, built in th' eclipse, and rigged with curses dark,
That sunk so low that sacred head of thine.

- John Milton (1608-1674)

A few hours after the eclipse, a 6.0 earthquake rocked the United States. It "woke up" people from northern Idaho to southern California. The eclipse had been preceded by deadly tornado outbreaks - plus a spate of shootings at schools and malls, not to mention ice storms, and floods. Is there more to come? Here's what I know for sure:

"Hope is a good breakfast, but it is a bad supper."

- Francis Bacon (1561-1626)

Miss Garcia, take a "Message of Caution" to the Generation of "Hope":

"Dear young Americans:

"I'm an old-timer. My father was born a long time ago. I come from a long line of farmers. You don't want to hear about that stuff, because you think that the future is 'what it's all about'! But what would you know? You will never know how much your Freedom cost my generation. I hope you will make good use of it!

"Very truly,

John Quincy Adams (1767-1848)

"P.S. Think of your forefathers! Think of your posterity!"

You're going to see a lot of those dates with the dashes in between in this book, because that's what our lives are - just a "dash" between the years (to paraphrase someone). My mother and father were born barely 50 years after John Quincy Adams died. Can you comprehend that? I have a brother who just turned 76, and - if you go back 76 years from the day our father was born, you are in the year 1824 - and your President is? The answer is: James Monroe!

John Quincy Adams was elected President that year, and Thomas Jefferson and Adams the elder were still alive! "Shocking," isn't it? Only 52 years separated the birth of my father from the lifetime of John Quincy Adams - and he was old enough at the time of the Declaration of Independence to remember it! What this all means is that America is too young to die, even if time flies when you're having fun, and fifty years in time is a nanosecond. We will all be history someday soon, so what do you want on your Tombstone?

What wee gave, we have;
What wee spent, wee had;
What wee kept, wee lost.

- Epitaph of the Earl of Devon (died 1419)

"LIFE IS A PARADOX," and the vocabulary of the general population has shrunk so much in the past 50 years that most kids wouldn't know the difference between a paradox and an irony, or the difference between a paradox and a parachute, but it pays to know what it is! A "paradox" is any concept that is "seemingly self-contradictory" (at least to some people), "but in reality is expressing a possible truth." Many a paradox was not recognized as a reality until it was too late (even though us geezers could have "told you so"). To translate that for our intellectuals: Many a "cognitive dissonance" was in truth a bell tolling for you a warning that a predictable reality was just waiting to happen!

"All is flux."

- Aristotle (384-322 B.C.)

"Democracy passes into despotism."

- Plato (429-347 B.C.)

One of the most valuable lessons that I learned from my mother was the value of the "dumb" question asked at just the right time, and here's a question that she would probably ask today :

"If President Kennedy warned us NOT to ask what our country can "do for us," why is nearly everyone asking what the government can DO for us now?"

This hip generation is just "a dash between the years," but they don't have a thought between the ears. They wouldn't know their History from a hole in the ground, or their Posterity from their posteriors!

How am I doing so far? With opening lines, you never know, but that reminds me of a story. I once met a single lady and said to her, "My first car was a Studebaker." She smiled and said, "Mine was too!" As opening lines go, that's called hitting a triple at my age.

Henry Aaron says, "The most exciting play in baseball is the triple." I saw Hank play in the first month of his career, and he's been in the Hall of Fame for decades. I once had a boss who had flown a Jenny in World War I - no joke - I'm in the seventh decade of my life, so I ask: "Do you ever wonder where you will be many years from now?"

> "Nae man can tether time nor tide."
> - Robert Burns (1759-1796)

> "The trouble with our age is all signpost and no destination."
> - Louis Kronenberger

When I was 60, I was standing atop the Grand Teton in Wyoming, from which I snapped that cover photo of Mt. Teewinot (if the background looks smoky, that's because the south wind was blowing in smoke from fires in Colorado and Arizona). By the way, that's 8,000 feet from the summit to Jenny Lake, a mile-and-a-half almost straight down. My first book had the same cover photo, but I used it again because I expect that more people will see it this time.

This book really ought to be required reading for younger Americans. My first, it was said, was "too difficult to understand" for them, although how to get pregnant and kill the baby seems to have been easier to understand. "It's time to stand athwart history and yell STOP," Bill Buckley used to say.

"Read the best books first" and climb your mountains while you can, because time is short. A kid once asked me, "How do you spell 'dummy'?" This untoward generation can't think outside the boxer shorts that they show off to the world. The only "dates" they ever care about happen on Saturday night. They can't stay awake in school, so what do they know anyway?

> And all to leave what with his toil he won
> To that unfeather'd two-legged thing, a son...
> Resolv'd to ruin or to rule the state.
>
> - John Dryden (1631-1700)

That guy died over 300 years ago, but you'll be reading a lot of those old "lines" in this book. Here's another gem from Dryden:

> For those whom God to ruin has design'd,
> He fits for fate, and first destroys their mind.

A more modern version of that was the song with the words that went, "Walk right in. Set yourself down. Do you want to lose your mind?" With "bummers" like those, I may've already lost some of my readers, but as Benjamin Disraeli (1804-1881), in his maiden speech to Parliament said:

> "Though I sit down now, the time will come when you will hear me."

There was a famous writer in Sweden, Carl Fredrik Dahlgren (1791-1844), who looked more like me than I do. He was a poet whose writings can still be read on the Internet (if you can read Swedish). [http://runeberg.org/cfd/] It is said that he was one of the most "famous" Nordic writers, though not necessarily the most "popular." That figures! The 11th edition of the Encyclopaedia Britannica says this:

"At a time when literary partisanship ran high in Sweden, and the writers divided themselves into 'Goths' and 'Phosphorists,' Dahlgren made himself indispensible to the Phosphorists by his polemical activity... In the mock-heroic poem of Markall's Sleepless Nights, in which the Phosphorists ridiculed the academician Per Adam Wallmark and others, Dahlgren, who was a genuine humorist, took a prominent part... Dahlgren is one of the best humorous writers that Sweden has produced; but he was perhaps at his best in realistic and idyllic description."

"O would that I could be so versatile! I can see that "literary partisanship" is running high again, and we need to find someone who could be so effective at "polemics" (if you want to look that word up in the dictionary, it stands right between polecat - skunk - and police state). My trusty '38 Funk & Wagnalls says that polemics is "the art of disputation or controversy."

By the way, what's the difference between a lawyer and a dead skunk in the middle of the road? The skunk has skid marks in front of it. You've probably heard that one before, but the lesson is: Maybe the only thing standing between the skunks in the middle of the road and a police state is "polemicism."

I don't know if I'm distantly related to Carl Dahlgren or not, but I do know that "polemical activity" runs in my veins, judging by my grampa Dahlgren's history. He spent a lot of time in the saloons - in disputation with socialists - and he wasn't the most popular guy in the saloon. Carl Dahlgren was a bit socialistic himself, but my point is: There is no "monopoly" worse than a school of thought that has a monopoly (like today's "Goths" in academe).

Jascha Heifetz said, "No matter what side of an argument you're on, you always find some people on your side that you wish were on the other side," and don't laugh, but Spiro T. Agnew once said, quite prophetically I might add:

"A spirit of national masochism prevails, encouraged by an effete corps of impudent snobs who characterize themselves as intellectuals."

I saw Ann Coulter speak at Northern Michigan University recently, and a handful of rascally radicals walked out early, going so far as to hurl obscenities at their guest speaker. These are the true colors of those who "characterize themselves" as intellectuals, though they haven't even bothered to consider what Ann is saying! I don't feel much "love" there. I sense a lot of anger there!

> "We can never be sure that the opinion we are endeavouring to stifle is a false opinion; and if we were sure, stifling it would be an evil still."
>
> - John Stuart Mill (1806-1873)

> "He that wrestles with us strengthens our nerves, and sharpens our skill."
>
> - Edmund Burke (1729-1797)

First, Some Defining Terminology:

"Polemics" and "polarization" come from the same root word, of course, but if you want the antonym of "polemics," it's one-sidedness. That means "considering only one side of a matter or question with all the advantage on one side." That's a better word for Academia today than partisan. It is all the rage these days to speak of "non-partisanship," but only as long as YOUR side has "all the advantage"" We, on the other hand, are always told to "stifle" ourselves, like Edith Bunker was always told. Screw that!

History teaches us that "polarization" doesn't lead to a police state, but a monopoly of one-sidedness almost invariably does. There is nothing to fear from discussion, least of all, the fear of contradiction. The root word for "history" simply meant "knowledge," and came from the Greek word "histor," or learned man (but there's a big difference between propaganda and real learning).

When Did Freedom Of Conscience Become A Thing Of The Past?

Tolerance is the new code-word for "stifle yourself." The pseudo-intellectuals "condemn" anyone who has a conscience that "judges righteous judgment," but isn't "condemnation" worse still? That sounds a lot like "hypocrisy," doesn't it?

Speaking of knowledge, "science" is the last word in conscience, which originally meant simply "to know together" or to be mutually aware, or to know something within oneself, and a parallel word is conscious - the concept of awareness – like, awareness of one's "ROOTS," eh?

"Conservative" is a most interesting word because Latin servare meant "to keep" or preserve. This root word also produced praeservare, or "to guard in advance." Thus a conservative is one who uses history and opinions to guard the Traditions that are worthy of preservation. Although a few Traditions aren't worth keeping, most are culturally important to your future. There's a Culture War going on right under your nose, which brings us to the word "nihilism."

Nihilism, n; 1) total rejection of value statements or moral judgments, 2) absolute destructiveness toward the world at large or oneself [nothingness, as in "nil" or ZERO]

So, the title of this book is a takeoff on "Letter to a Christian Nation" by Sam Harris. That book was a crudely researched attempt to insult the common sense of the American people, and so is the writing of the Englishman Richard Dawkins. As I will show, however, their "scholarship" is an even greater insult to our Common Heritage, and to our Identity!

> ... I think I may call
> Their belief a belief in nothing at all,
> Or something of that sort; I know they went
> For a general union of total dissent.
>
> - James Russell Lowell (1819-1891)

One might say that this book wasn't "written"; it sort of "evolved," as if pounded out by billions and billions of monkeys on billions and billions of keyboards (ha ha). But seriously though, putting this book together was almost like assembling a 10,000-piece jigsaw puzzle, and you probably won't see the "Big Picture" until you finish reading it, so hang in there.

A LITTLE CONTEXT, PLEASE: my father saw Buffalo Bill, and he heard a speech by Roosevelt - I mean Teddy - when he was running for President (and Teddy's been on Mount Rushmore for over 65 years already)! My friends call me the Old Man (and they're the only kids I have). I'm writing for them because I fear for their future, a future in which "work" is a 4-letter word, and words such as "God" will mean zip, zero - nothing!

In the cell phone era, books are totally gonzo, but maybe someone will "hear me now." As for "work," the liberals who think that "The Ugly American" was a great book are the same people who now tell us that we can't guard our borders because we're so wealthy that there are "jobs Americans won't do." With an attitude as ugly as that, we could end up with the opposite problem, no jobs at all.

On the planet I came from, words and work went together. My parents worked from before sunrise on the farm to after sundown, but they were still avid readers and news junkies, and in the early 1940s, my family had two great acquisitions. My mother and dad obtained one of the last Massey-Harris 101 Jr.s built before World War II - and a new son to drive it.

I was "born to raise hay." I don't even want to say how young I was when I started driving that tractor. Let's put it this way: I know a farm girl who started steering her dad's tractor at the age of four, and I knew how to drive a tractor and a truck before I learned how to ride a bike (this was not unusual; our parents would've had a hard time keeping us out of the "driver's seat"). The bottom line is that "work" is what gave us our satisfaction; we had more "self-esteem" than the city kids (then or now).

By the way, mountain guides in Wyoming say that kids who can successfully climb the Grand Teton have done things with their fathers! Last year I was talking to a young man and asked him what his dad did for a living. He named the company he works for, and I asked him what they make. He said that he didn't know, because his dad had never told him. Apparently he wasn't even interested enough to ask either! I knew what my dad made! Since I was old enough to walk almost, I was in the same business. I don't have any memories from age 3 about the house we lived in, but I can remember the cow barn!

When we moved from Illinois to Wisconsin (where the house was part log cabin), we made milk, beef, eggs, chicken, duck, goose, and even had a few guineas and pigs. We made maple syrup, buckwheat, logs, vegetables, and firewood, and made a dollar-a-pound for minnows that we trapped in the creek. I've done almost all of those jobs that "Americans won't do," including butchering, picking cucumbers, washing dishes, and scrubbing toilets. Oh, and we also had a flock of sheep to shear, which reminds me of the old proverb, "You can shear a sheep as long as it lives, but you can only skin it once."

Speaking of the creek, to go bring the cows home, I would run as fast as I could across the rocks in the creek and on top of the bogs. They didn't come at regular spaces, so you had to be quick to hit the next bog. Walking behind the cows in the barn also helped me develop what is called a "quick first step." If you saw a cow with her tail up and she was taking a deep breath, you knew that a cough was coming, and you had to be quick if you were standing behind her. Something was about to hit the fan. There's probably a lesson in there somewhere. Enough about me, but if you're looking for a line to take out of context, try this one:

My mother never asked us to help do the dishes, and we never asked her to help us pitch manure. Life on the farm was sort of "funny," but it was no "riddle"; what had to be done, you did it! When it was cold outside, you just put on more clothes, and we knew that the chicken came first. I mean, all the animals came first on the day's "to do" list. We had it memorized.

By the way, because the animals come first, farmers develop a keen sense of hearing. They have to be acutely aware of any signs of discomfort in a cow or other animal, as that's a sign that they've been forgotten, or it could mean a disease coming on. Ex-farmers make the best pet caretakers, because farming increases the sense of awareness of "what is wrong with this picture."

More about that later, but life on the farm was almost all work and no play. We may have been "dull," but we weren't stupid. Kindergarten was cut to just six weeks in those days to give kids more time to do farm work, but - at the cost of a pittance - they taught us how to READ in six weeks (with the phonetic method, of course). It would never have occurred to any of us then (not even the "duller" kids) that someday kids wouldn't even be able to read diplomas, let alone comic books (for which we had no use).

I mean, I was so "culturally deprived" that I had never heard of a snow angel until around age 40, and I never had the time to watch "The Wizard of Oz" until I was about 40 years old (most of it is overrated anyway, except the part about needing a brain)! That may sound "mean-spirited," but I'm not being entirely facetious.

My first really BIG lessons in life were learned behind the wheel of that Massey-Harris 101 Jr. At one mile per hour, cultivating corn on cornrows nearly a half-mile long was the "video game" of our times, but I neither heard nor uttered the word boring until many years later (and I still can't understand the concept). We had never heard the term "sleeping in" and we walked over a mile to school (as opposed to walking a mile in your shoes around "the mall" today). By the way, in grade school there were no bullies, basketballs, or drive-by shootings.

Truancy was an unknown concept, too, although one of my uncles once killed a skunk on the way to school, and there's a joke about "little Johnny" arriving late one day. When the teacher wanted to know the reason, he said, "The road was so icy and the wind was blowing so hard that for every step forward I took two steps back."

The teacher looked at him with that classic "cross" look, and so he says, "Finally I decided to walk backwards and here I am!" Even if he didn't have an "excuse," we're talking about the Good old days and he understood logic and arithmetic. Two plus two equaled four in those days!

"What I Did Last Summer" - 1950s style:

"I learned a lot last summer. Lesson #1: Cultivating corn for 8-9 hours a day at 1 or 2 mph can be a wonderful experience. You wonder how the seed knows how to make the corn grow UP instead of down. Then you wonder how high is up, and which way that really is! Then you see a red-tailed hawk circling and you wonder about the birds and the bees - and how anyone can believe that this all evolved. You wonder how the birds could survive before wings or worms, or how the bees survived without the flowers.

"You wonder which came first, the omasum or the abomasum of a cow, and since man's digestive system needs an entrance and an exit, you wonder which came first. If we evolved ever so "gradually," there could have been people who were "all mouth," - or people who were all rectum (those must have been the world's first evolutionists).

"Lesson # 2: When harvesting the corn in August, you wonder how it is possible that dirt can produce a nearly 10-feet-tall flagpole with all those green flags and a gold ornament at the top? You wonder how this field can yield tons and tons of crop year after year without sinking. How is that possible?

"Then I was looking at the clouds, trying to find interesting shapes, and I noticed the red-tailed hawk being chased by blackbirds or crows. One begins to wonder what really causes war, but then my dad came to get me, because it was time for the cows to come home. On the longest days of summer, I'd always hit a few baseballs up the hill behind the house, and watched as it rolled back to me.

"In the evening, my brother would take me to the mill to go for a swim, and as I watched the water going over the dam, I wondered, Who invented gravity - or its opposite - levity? And I slept well that night. One night, I had a dream, and I dreamed that I climbed Jacob's ladder (way out into outer space, beyond the moon). When I looked down, I couldn't even see the earth anymore.

"Lesson #3: After hoeing potatoes one day, I laid the hoe down, and it hit me: we 'dirt farmers' know which came first, the chicken or the egg, and we didn't need to be too bright. Obviously, it was the chicken (because the chicken could always lay the egg, but the egg could never lay the chicken). I had a lot of fun hoeing last summer, but I can't wait to learn more about history, and I think I know Who "invented" Light! Without Light, we wouldn't even be able to SEE each other, let alone multiply."

"What I Did Last Summer" - version 2008:

"While we be hangin and lissnin to muzic last summr, we lernt a lot of lessans. We be lernin how to get to get to 1st base, how to get to 2nd base, how to get to 3rd base, and how to make a inside da park home run, yknow? But the ho turned out to be a ******* ***** [I forget the words]! She be dissin me now so I be stayin in skul jus long enuf to fine me a nu ho to lay. Not having a ho to lay is a real nightmare."

The only thing some thugs use a baseball bat for today is to beat people to death, and whether urban or suburban, our kids today are worse off than the Scarecrow. His silo didn't have a roof on it, and he was a few brain cells short of a full wheel barrow, but (did you know?) there's a tiny creature that lives in the lips of the North Atlantic lobsters, species Symbion pandora, which is "unique" in that its BRAIN COMPLETELY DISAPPEARS during adolescence. It's not that unique though, since this happens to almost every teenager (I can remember like it was yesterday). What makes this pandora nearly unique is that its brain reappears at adulthood.

Some kids today never do grow up! They know their rights of course, and have "self-esteem," but without role models, they never quite comprehend the concept of "irresponsibility." It's probably not even on today's spelling lists (since irresponsibility has seven syllables). I think that the limit is now about two. Some teachers can't even spell "potato" or "quayle." Sorry about that, Dan, but my ghost writer is on strike, and I'm making these up as I go (hope it was the Scarecrow that needed the brain).

Hey – how about a "right to read and write"? That would do more to promote responsible behavior than all the "remedial education" in the world. The mother of a public school kid complained that one of the kids had gotten away with a blatantly irresponsible act. She said, "We need to teach kids today that for every right there's a responsibility." The teacher was shocked and said, "You can't do that!"

"CONCLUSIONS" ANYONE? The last item in Pandora's box was hope, but in and of itself, "hope" is useless. We didn't have much "diversity" in that school, but after six week's worth of kindergarten and one summer of driving that Massey-Harris 101, I had learned just about everything I needed to know about the "survival of the fittest."

Our teacher, Mrs. Splittgerber, certainly thought that she could teach us a thing or two about work and responsibility! When she told you to go downstairs and get a bucket of coal for the stove, she didn't "hope" that you would obey her. You didn't tell her that that's "a job most Americans don't do" (because we didn't have so many lawyers in those days). Burke once said that:

> "It's not what a lawyer tells me I can do; it's what my conscience tells me I must do!"

I'm paraphrasing, but the exact quote will come later. Some things bear repeating and this book has more than one repetition. Repeating oneself is an occupational hazard for a writer as old as Colonel Sanders was when he started "Kentucky Fried," but most of my "reps" are intentional.

"Good writers are monotonous, like good composers. Their truth is self-repeating… They keep trying to perfect their understanding of the one problem they were born to understand."

- Alberto Moravia

Saul Bellow said, "You never have to change anything you got up in the middle of the night to write." Much of this book was written between 2 and 4 o'clock in the morning, the time of the the day when that "one big problem" comes into sharpest focus: we can't admit a mistake! Dr. Benjamin Spock admitted that his theories were all wrong before he died. WHY CAN'T WE?

"In reality there is perhaps no one of our natural Passions so hard to subdue as Pride. Disguise it, struggle with it, beat it down, stifle it, mortify it as much as one pleases, it is still alive."

- Ben Franklin

We didn't use the McGuffey Readers, but we recited the Pledge of Allegiance at Duck Creek School. I would do my workbook assignments as fast as I could so I could listen to all the lessons that the older kids were being given, and my ears especially perked up when history was involved. I calculate that I thus got about 64 years' worth of history and six weeks of kindergarten (I repeat) in nine years. And the American Bible Society handed out New Testaments to all of us. The "role of religion in our country's history" wasn't too complicated to understand. When "under God" was added to the Pledge, not one of us was "offended."

"Religion and good morals are the only solid foundation of public liberty and happiness."

- Samuel Adams (1778)

Today there's a misunderstanding about the so-called "Wall of Separation" between religion and State. It's a myth, essentially. The Founders feared control of religion by the State – and control of local affairs by a overly "ambitious" central government - a lot more than control of the State by religion (some people would ban believers from voting - if they could)! The Founding Fathers preached "separation of England and America," not separation of religion from the public square.

Patrick Henry was standing in a church, in fact, when he made his "Give me liberty or give me death" speech (at the Second Virginia Convention in 1775). Of course there was no official denomination such as the Church of England (thank God), but the Founders never threatened to make preachers shut up about political issues. They encouraged and cultivated a spirit of involvement - by all the people, even the clergy - although some lawyers were evidently "jealous of their territory" even in those days. As the old Puritan, John Adams, said:

"If a clergyman preaches Christianity, and tells magistrates that they are not distinguished from their [fellow citizens] for their private [benefit], but for the good of the people... Oh sedition! treason!" To paraphrase Patrick Henry, "If this be treason, make the most of it."

John Eidsmoe says, "Adams' Puritan ancestors had insisted that they were engaged in an effort to establish a new and purified religious community founded on the teachings of the Bible...[and] Adams, in a similar spirit, insisted that [the Founders] were concerned with establishing a new and purified kind of political community, founded on the Christian religion and the precepts of John Locke [etc]."

John Jay [the first Chief Justice of the Supreme Court!] gave a speech in 1776 in New York urging the ratification of the Constitution, a speech filled with words about Jacob, Esau, and Nebuchadnezzar, and he made the point that, "Even the Jews, those favourites of Heaven, met with frowns, when they forgot the smiles of their benevolent Creator."

Jay once said that "even a dead body can float downstream." If we don't start going against the grain, against the "mainstream," Freedom will become an anachronistic, archaic relic of the past. I can't help but conclude that, in the past half century, the proliferation of drugs, crime, and "deadbeat-dadism" has been directly proportional to the growth in the number of lawyers we have.

> "Then, shifting his side, (as a lawyer knows how)… "
> - William Cowper (1731-1800)

A lawyer goes to confession and he says: "I wish to confess the sin of vanity. Every time I look in the mirror, I think how handsome I am." The priest, who recognized the voice and knew what the guy looked like, says: "That's not a sin. That's a mistake!"

BINGO. That's why we can't admit a mistake: VANITY. To admit a "mistake" would hurt our "self-esteem," and we all know how important that is today, don't we? Self-esteem trumps even the most obvious solutions, and kids are being controlled by "the same hormones that cause pimples"! I know, there are some good teachers out there, but their hands are tied by the powers-that-be.

If an elementary teacher today told a kid to go get a bucket of coal, or an armful of wood, he would probably swear and tell her to go get it herself, because he "knows his rights." Our Mrs. Splittgerber would've just grabbed a pointer or a ruler, and said, "I wasn't born yesterday, you know!"

"There I go again." I generalize about kids, but - no matter what the lawyer class says - there are some problems we just don't need to put up with! And I didn't end that sentence with a preposition, either; I ended it with an exclamation point! By the way, did you know that "tolerance" really means "bearing" or "putting up with?" Mrs. Splittgerber was all business, and she didn't "put up with" monkeyshines.

What I'm getting around to is the fact that most of today's kids wouldn't know a "preposition" from a "proposition." The latter is a much higher priority, and if they're children already having children, they think they've "done it all, seen it all, and HEARD it all"!

Nor rural sights alone, but rural sounds,
Exhilarate the spirit, and restore
The tone of languid Nature...
God made the country, and man made the town.

- William Cowper

"The country life is to be preferred, for there we see the works of God, but in cities little else but the works of men."

- William Penn (1644-1718)

"But God has a few of us whom [He] whispers in the ear... The C Major of this life."

- Robert Browning (1812-1889)

- Introduction to the Introduction -

"A LETTER TO GENERATION XYZ"

> "The words of the wise are as cattle prods."
> - The wisest man of his time, Solomon

Dear Gen XYZers:

I'm an old geezer. You probably feel sorry for us guys and hope we just "move along" so we don't hog all the Social Security money you need for your "disabilities" (due to addictions). As for drugs, you've probably done 'em all, but we're sick and tired of paying for your drugs when we can hardly afford a bottle of aspirin! "And besides that":

YOU THINK YOU'VE JUST ABOUT DONE IT ALL? Ha! I feel "sorry" for you!

If you think that crap music is awesome, but you've never heard the corn grow, or total silence - I'm sorry about that, but you ain't heard "nothin" yet!

If you think that shooting up is "awesome," but you've never smelled the approach of a much-needed thunderstorm still over the horizon, you ain't done nothin' yet.

Curtis Dahlgren

If you think that snorting stuff is awesome, but you've never experienced the smell of new-mown hay, sorry about that; you haven't done zilch!

If you think that Hollywood skin flicks are awesome, but you've never seen a pair of bald eagles swooping across the water one foot above the river, you ain't seen nothin' yet.

If you think that a Hollywood seduction scene is awesome, but you've never seen a female wolf trying to lure your own dog across the river and into the woods, you ain't seen squat!

If you think that Hollywood premiers or the Oscars are exciting, but you've never helped deliver a newborn calf, you ain't done nothin' yet.

If you think that illegal drugs are awesome, but you've never tasted home-made maple syrup, or the sweet part of a clover blossom, I'm sorry about that!

If you think that getting 'high' is awesome, but you've never climbed to the top of a 14,000-foot mountain, I'm very sorry 'bout that.

If you think that MTV or big TVs are cool, but you've never climbed a silo, or a redwood tree, you ain't done nothin' - yet.

If you think that the latest man-made electronic devices are awesome, but you've never seen a flock of migrating monarch butterflies resting in the bushes, sorry about that.

If you think that comedians who mock "the man" are awesome, but you have never heard a mockingbird mock one of your own whistles, you ain't heard nothin' yet.

If you think Volvos or BMWs are awesome, but you've never seen a pileated woodpecker tearing big chunks out of a dead tree, I have to say, "You ain't seen nothin' yet."

If you think a Hummer H3 is awesome, but you've never communicated with a hummingbird outside your window via hand signals, sorry about that!

If you think that getting a driver's license is cool, but you've never seen a gathered flock of eagles and had one flying so close in front of your car that he's almost a hood ornament, you ain't got much to brag about!

If you think that a space shuttle blast-off is awesome, but you've never heard the WHOOSH of the wings of an eagle taking off from a branch a few feet above you, you ain't heard nothin' yet.

If you think that the international space station is awesome, but you've never spent 3 or 4 days in the Boundary Waters listening to loons, you ain't done nothin' yet..

If you think the landing of a Martian land-rover is awesome, but you've never seen a road runner gliding to a landing, you ain't done zilch.

If you think that "hangin' out in the 'hood" is awesome, but you've never walked across a beaver dam and watched a beaver swimming along with a five-foot log, you ain't seen nothin'.

If you think that "hip-hop" is what's happening, but you've never seen badgers in the wild, or never watched otters running on the river and belly-flopping on the ice, sorry for you!

If you think that "cruising chicks" is cool, but you've never been driving down the road and seen a bald eagle chasing a mallard duck in mid-air (and rescued the duck by distracting them), you ain't seen nothin' "cool"!

You think she thinks you're so COOL, but if you've never found a bear den, never seen a 60-inch muskie, never pullled a rattlesnake out of the ground with your bare hands, nor shined a flashlight into the eyes of a bear, I'm not impressed.

If you think that a teen-aged "score" is a high, but you've never thrown a curve ball, or hit a pinch-hit triple in a hardball game, you ain't done nothing, Jack!

If you think Las Vegas and San Francisco are awesome, but you've never seen Niagara Falls - or the world's largest tree - you ain't seen nothing!.

If you think the city life is "what's up," but you've never looked up at the sky and seen stars so dazzling that you almost got whiplash, you ain't seen nothin' yet!

If you think that cell phones are awesome, but you've never been lost in the North Woods where cell phones don't work, nor compasses (because of the iron in the ground), and got a glimpse of the sun through the clouds just long enough to know True North, you ain't done anything at all!

You think you're so blasted COOL, but if you never finished S-COOL, or gotten around to knowing your Creator, dittos that!

I've been there, done that, all of those things! I may be old and part "hick," but I'll tell you one thing: I graduated from high school. If you ain't even done that, what have you really "DONE" yet? To use the correct word this time, you haven't done much of anything at all, so what makes you think you're cool, or that Youth "rules"?

I hate to tell you, but - Youth doesn't "rule." The Law of Nature rules! The day I got lost in northern Minnesota, I was really, really "lost" - and I believe quite factually that the God of Nature and of my Forefathers opened up the sky for three seconds or so, just enough to enable me to find True North, and get to a road by dead reckoning. Otherwise, I would have had to spent a very cold night out in the national forest.

Incidentally, the reason I got lost was my own fault - for "doing something stupid" (I didn't mark the trail I came in on, which would have allowed me to retrace my footsteps). For those who hate history, there might be a lesson in there for you someplace. America needs to retrace her footsteps. As someone once said:

"God forgives; man sometimes forgives; Nature never forgives!"

Yours truly,
The Old Man

P.S. If you finish school: Find True North and come UP and see me sometime. Let me show you around the 'hood. You never know what you might be able to see. Just yesterday, my neighbor was telling me about a day he spent fishing near my house last summer.

He was standing in the middle of the river near an island and had caught three nice fish when all of a sudden he noticed a black bear drinking water and watching him from the right bank. He immediately looked left and saw a doe and a fawn on the other bank. At that instant, he sensed something overhead. He looked up and it was a huge American bald eagle cruising by. All that had happened within a few seconds, and he said he felt the biggest rush he had ever felt in his life (he had given up illicit drugs a few years ago). Wouldn't that make a great scene in a movie? Hollywood could call it "Finding True North" or "Massey-Harris 101." And here's another possible scene:

Last week, a friend by the name of Chris was allowed to go along with a biologist to help weigh bear cubs while their mothers were hibernating. Now that must be a RUSH. So, come UP and visit me sometime. We have plenty of room (the Upper Peninsula has 340,000 acres for every man, woman, and child who lives here). "UP here, it's a great place for the RACE - the human race!"

PPS: Who'd you think I was writing this to? I've been called "white bread" before, but I write for the website of a 'black' American (a real man who would probably rather be called "just an American."

"I don't care if the cat is black or white - so long as it's a good mouser."

- author anon.

- *Introduction* -

"THINKING OUTSIDE THE BOXER SHORTS"

"Few in their after years have occasion to change their college opinions."

— Thomas Jefferson

"Freedom is never more than one generation away from extinction. We didn't pass it to our children in the bloodstream."

— Ronald Reagan

NEVER MIND, FOR THE MOMENT, whether my opinions are "too opinionated." I know it's not cool to be "too certain" about certain subjects - although the "elitists" are more than willing to silence all discussion regarding other subjects, such as, Darwinism and climate change ("man made").

PR spin or "Just the facts, ma'am?" I want a second opinion, because, as General George Patton said, "If everybody is thinking alike, someone isn't thinking."

Not to interrupt my own "rambling," but if you are a green and/or secular college professor, you might as well just go on the end of the book to see how it turns out. Or, you might just use this book for kindling the next time they turn your lights out and "the party's over," due to your own stupid energy policies - on nuclear power and drilling for oil, for example. Before you throw this book into the fire, though, I want you to take a look at "Section 2"!

Up here, we are not intimidated by the phony "hockey-stick graph" that you nerds concocted to illustrate "the carbon problem" (the aim of which is more to milk money from the taxpayer for your own benefit than to "save the planet"). And "my point" IS:

The REAL "hockey-stick graph" is the one William Bennett called the Index of Leading Cultural Indicators, to quantify the rise in social problems such as divorce, crime, and 'school dropoutism' since the 1960s. And if you go back to the year I was born, 1942, America's divorce rate was only two percent! Worst of all, the value of human life on the "world market" has gone down like an upside-down hockey-stick

We can shoot a man from Milwaukee to the moon and bring him back safely (the commander of Apollo 13), but you can't deliver a pizza in Milwaukee without getting shot dead! Even one of our astronauts was arrested for contemplating violence, and I have personally lost eight close friends in Milwaukee to murder.

Some of my younger readers may not even realize that murder used to be uncommon. The 1957 Yankees called Milwaukee "Bush League" during the World Series, but there was a lot more crime in New York than in Milwaukee in those days (its police were the "finest"). Since most of the country sold out and surrendered to the cosmopolitan philosophies of the intelligentsia, even Milwaukee is now a war zone.

I lived there for a couple of years, part of the time on north 36th Street, where today you can't walk down the street in broad daylight without fear for your life. We have seen the future, and it's what's happening now. There is no joy in Mudville, nor Pigville, because the Mighty Casey has struck out. Our "justice system" is a joke. We have gotten God out of the schools - and replaced Him with what? We not only have serial killers now, but I think we have serial demons out there (don't look so shocked; two-thirds of Americans still believe that the devil is real.)

During the few weeks I was finalizing this manuscript, there were school shootings at Memphis, Baton Rouge, Oxnard, and DeKalb. There were two recent church shootings in Colorado, and 3,000 people in Reno attended the funeral for a beautiful young lady who was kidnapped, and raped, and murdered. Another eight students were just shot in Jerusalem (and Hamas hailed the "heroic" action). So much for "the Goodness of the Human Spirit," eh Mr. Harris? Certain policies cultivate and encourage anarchy and death, so let's deal in facts, not hedonistic cliches such as "God is dead" or "global warming," or "you can't legislate morality."

"Public schools 'tis public folly feeds."

- William Cowper

"You can't legislate morality," said a comic strip once, "But immorality is easy!" So the "word-for-the-day," boys and girls is BANDY. The anti-Traditionalist segment of society is at war with the rest of us and they bandy about lies, damned lies, statistics, and "polls" to try to propagandize the rest of us. These "secularists" lie - about everything from homelessness to the percentage of homosexuals in our population - and they ignore our really big problems. Can you say bandy, boys and girls? I want you to pay attention now - because you're going to be quizzed on this later:

"To 'bandy words with someone' may go back to an original idea of 'banding together to oppose others.' The word comes from French bander (oppose). The rather complex semantic development goes from 'taking sides' to 'opposing a third party' to 'exchanging blows' to 'hitting a ball back and forth, in tennis,' to 'exchanging hostile words.' Furthermore: "The adjective bandy (as in 'bandy legs') probably comes from the noun bandy, a curved stick used in an early form of hockey (also known as 'bandy')."

This is the point I was born to make: "An attack on your ROOTS is an attack on YOU." The anti-Traditionalists are just playing mind-games with us. You have been hustled by pimps. There is truly "nothing new under the sun," not even the "hockey-stick graph" of global warming.

R. Buckminster Fuller said, "Pollution is nothing but resources we're not harvesting." His point isn't exactly clear, but oil does come from the ground, you know, and the less oil we pump out of the ground, the more oil that the earth spews into the oceans. I heard a guy say, "The reason the earth is warming up is because we're pumping oil out of the ground and the earth's axelrod is getting hot." But scientists can't even say for sure whether the earth is warming or cooling.

OF ALL THE QUOTATIONS in this book, the following one by Abba Eban may be my favorite of all time:"A consensus is when we all agree to say in public what none of us would say in private." He also said:

> "Propaganda is the art of persuading others of what one does not believe oneself."

THE WHEAT AND THE CHAFF: We used to say that there are "two sides to the coin," so I wonder whatever happened to "Sifting and winnowing the Truth" in the University? Bacon said:

> "The inquiry of truth, which is the love-making, or wooing of it, the knowledge of truth, which is the presence of it, and the belief of truth, which is the enjoying of it, is the sovereign good of human nature... If a man will begin with certainties, he shall end in doubts; but if he will be content to begin with doubts, he shall end in certainties.... The knowledge of man is as the waters, some descended from above, and some springing from beneath; the one informed by the light of nature, the other inspired by divine revelation."

"Some drink deeply from the river of knowledge. Others only gargle." I think Tennyson said that, but my nomination for worst-quote-of-the-century goes to Shimon Peres, who said, "It is a great mistake to learn from history. There is nothing to learn from history." [May 23, 1996]

> "History is philosophy teaching by examples."
> - "Dion" (40-08 B.C.)

If you've never heard of Dionysius or Francis Bacon, maybe that's because the modern "book burners" on the Left have almost banned the history of Western Civilization from our public schools. If he were alive today, a William Shakespeare wouldn't be able to get his name into his local paper's obituary column without a public relations consultant, an agent, and a writers union rep. All is flux, fun and games, and the "Times" they are a'changin' (the London and New York Times, that is). Given the dominant left-wing attitudes of the universities and the "journalists" they produce, Shakespeare today would probably have to peddle his writings door-to-door. Tragically, as the late Daniel Patrick Moynihan once said:

> "To strip our past of glory is no great loss, but to deny it honor is devastating."

If it were necessary to combine history with some other subject, it would have been wiser to combine it with Classical Literature and "religion appreciation" classes than with "social science" and biology. There was a relative consistency of thought in Western literature, especially in the English-speaking world, from the 1500s to the 1950s. Even if not unanimously held to, our foundational Cultural values produced progress for both science and human rights - slowly but surely - so long as those principles were honored and remembered!

> "Every drop of the Thames is liquid 'istory."
> - John Burns (1858-1943)

Anthony Flew was 80-something when, after years and years of atheistic philosophizing, he admitted in 2005 to believing now in a First Cause or a Designer. Like Alex Haley, he went back to his roots. He had been reared Methodist, and he said this about his spiritual forebears, John and Charles Wesley:

> "The greatest thing is their tremendous achievement of creating the Methodist movement mainly among the working class. Methodism made it impossible to build a really substantial Communist Party in Britain and provided the country with a generous supply of men and women of sterling moral character from mainly working class families. Its decline is a substantial part of the explosions both of unwanted motherhood and of crime in recent decades."

He also is in favor of "modest" efforts in the public schools that would allow kids to at least have a vague grasp of where they "came from," to paraphrase. I recommend reading his interview with Dr. Gary Habermas in 1985. Here's a link: http://theroadtoemmaus.org/RdLb/21PbAr/Apl/FlewTheist.htm

Flew says it's impossible to get any spirituality into the British schools anymore, but he still has some "hope" for America. I might add however, that Islam seems to be more "in" than the Wesleys! Thanks to John Dewey and others, Darwinism "rules" in the schools, and science and religion are made out to be – falsely so - enemies of one another (by comparing the best of science and the worst of religion). This is a Johnnie-come-lately strawman that's "BUL" (which in Olde English meant a "falsehood," a LIE). This strawman has no brain. Lord Tennyson (1809-1892) wrote:

> Let knowledge grow from more to more,
> But more reverence in us dwell;
> That mind and soul, according well,
> May make one music as before.

The power of personal prayer is still proven every day, but taxpayer money is being spent in the vain pursuit of "proving" Darwin's theory (about 150 years after he published Origin). We have more Intelligent Design proponents than ever, but the news media just don't care. They have unleashed a massive blitzkrieg against our past, our ROOTS, and our SOULS.

> I heard the old, old men say,
> 'All that's beautiful drifts away
> Like the waters.'
>
> - William Butler Yeats (1865-1939)

If history has anything to say, political correctness will also be the death of education, but as "the ayatollah of atheism" Richard Dawkins says, he wants to make belief in God "socially unacceptable." Is that not Orwellian, or what? That is quintessential Groupthink and Newspeak. "Sam Harris 101" teaches that in their Brave New World:

"At some point, there's going to be enough pressure that it is just going to be too embarrassing to believe in God." In his dreams! He must have missed "Massey-Harris 101." A nightmare for an atheist must be dreaming that there is a God, and I'd bet a dollar AND a donut that that happens a lot!

> "By night an atheist half believes a God."
> - Edward Young (1683-1765)

But follow the money: Where the big bucks are, in Big Education, your tax dollars aren't being used to actually create "diversity" (as is claimed). The High Priests and/or Priestesses on Campi (the hockey pucks) are working to create a MONO-CULTURE, 180 degrees opposed to the one that was cultivated by our Founding Fathers way back to the Magna Carta, which was inspired by our Judeo-Christian beliefs (for example, the God-given value of the Individual "created in the image of God").

Margaret Thatcher said, "A society needs only one generation to abandon... its culture, for that culture to become an alien, lifeless

Curtis Dahlgren

irrelevance... [and] the cultural revolutionaries will drown out what Lincoln called the 'mystic chords of memory' with jarring cacophony."

Michael Savage says, "We've gone from Beethoven to rap in one generation" Yes, we've gone from Mozart to anti-Christian arts in a virtual nanosecond. President Ronald Reagan said:

"The deliberations of great leaders and great bodies are but overture. The truly majestic music, the music of freedom, of justice, and peace is the music made in forgetting self and seeking in silence the will of Him who made us."

Does that make your "head hurt"? It might "shock" you even more if you knew that those words were President Reagan's parting advice to the UN General Assembly in his Farewell Address, but today's leaders cower before the ACLU, and allow our sworn enemies to come to New York City and mock America. They must think we have "nothing to learn from history."

Edmund Burke said: "People will not look forward to posterity, who never look backward to their ancestors," and the song Chuck Berry sang was: "Hail, hail rock and roll; deliver me from the days of old."

After 40 years of "rockin," Neil Young has just recently come to the conclusion that "music can't save the world." WELL DUH. HELL-OOO? Music can't even save "music."

Rush Limbaugh says, "If you want to 'save' something, save yourselves [not the planet]."

What difference does it make? There isn't much "difference" between laughter and slaughter, but it pays to know what it is! A lot of "plastic banana" rock n' rollers wouldn't be able to tell the difference between morality and immorality to save their lives. Most people certainly can't relate to our Founding Fathers. Is that just because of the white wigs and the breeches? No, I think it's because the Founders were so much more intelligent than Generation XYZ. There's a book entitled "What Would the Founders Do? (Our Questions, Their Answers)" by Richard Brookhiser, as reviewed by Michael Knox Beran (National Review, 6/19/06):

"We scrutinize the Founders' parchment for clues to guide our conduct today precisely because they were smart. Their 'talent level,' Brookhiser writes, was 'humiliatingly high'… Why were the Founders so smart? Possibly this 'greatest generation' of law-giving talent was the result of chance or providential dispensation." There's another concept that's totally foreign to too many of our "cool" kids. Is it apathy or ignorance? They don't know and don't care! George Washington, in his first Inaugural address, said:

"No people can be bound to acknowledge and adore the Invisible Hand which conducts the affairs of men more than those of the United States. Every step by which they have advanced to… an independent nation seems to have been distinguished by some token of providential agency… [and] can not be compared with the means by which most governments have been established without some return of pious gratitude, along with an humble anticipation of the future blessings which the past seem to presage. These reflections, arising out of the present crisis, have forced themselves too strongly on my mind to be suppressed…

"Since there is no truth more thoroughly established than that there exists in… nature an indissoluble union between virtue and happiness… since we ought to be no less persuaded that the propitious smiles of Heaven can never be expected on a nation that disregards the eternal rules of order and right which Heaven itself has ordained; and since the preservation of the sacred fire of liberty and the destiny of the republican model of government are justly considered, perhaps, as deeply, as finally, staked on the experiment intrusted to the hands of the American people…

"Having thus imparted to you my sentiments as they have been awakened by the occasion which brings us together, I shall take my present leave; but not without resorting once more to the benign Parent of the Human Race in humble supplication that, since He has been pleased to favor the American people with opportunities for deliberating in perfect tranquility, and dispositions for deciding with unparalleled unanimity on a form of government for the security of their union and the advancement of happiness, so His divine blessing may be equally conspicuous in the enlarged views, the temperate consultations, and the wise measures on which the success of this Government must depend."

Public education has been so dumbed down that it would now be impossible for most kids to make heads or tails out of the preceding paragraphs! A ninth-grade "language" teacher today would probably give the Father of our Country a "D-" for that last paragraph (which is all one sentence). She would probably write, "You use too many capital letters, the wording is quite antiquated, and why did you inject religion and nationalism? You can't do that!"

I've run into three grads of the high school I attended who didn't even know what the fourth of July commemorates. When given a clue, "England," they all said the same thing: "Beatles!" They didn't even know what the word "commemorates" means. By the way, if you didn't know this, Washington was our first President! He may have been the only President who took his oath of office on an opened Bible. There's some debate as to the chapter to which it was opened, but some say it was Deuteronomy 28, which talks about blessings and "cursings."

A Quotation for the Ages:

In his first Inaugural address, President James Monroe asked, "What has raised us to the present happy state?... The Government has been in the hands of the people. To the people, therefore, and to the faithful and able depositories of their trust is the credit due. Had the people … been less intelligent, less independent, or less virtuous, can it be believed that we should have… been blessed with the same success? While then [America] retains its sound and healthful state, everything will be safe. They will choose competent and faithful representatives…

"It is only when the people become ignorant and corrupt, when they degenerate into a populace, that they are incapable of exercising the sovereignty. Usurpation is then an easy attainment, and an usurper soon found. The people themselves become the willing instruments of their own debasement and ruin."

President Monroe concluded, like Washington and others, with a prayer to the Almighty "that He will be graciously pleased to continue to us that protection which He has already so conspicuously displayed in our favor."

Probably not a single soul was "offended" that day, but now prayer is slowly but surely being banned from the public square! Skeptics charge that the Founders didn't actually use the word "God," but (a) that's just a generic word anyway; (b) they didn't believe in using His name in vain. As for scattered atheists who might be "offended" at the mention of God, Jefferson said:

"The legitimate powers of government extend to such acts only as are injurious to others. But it does me no injury for my neighbour to say there are twenty gods, or no god. It neither picks my pocket nor breaks my leg."

Highlight that and get this: Banning the mention of God's name is no more a legitimate power of our government than banning the utterance "Mother Nature" (and no" pledge of allegiance" ever broke a leg). But the ACLU thinks that God is finally dead and the "equal rights" of some are more equal than others. All is hopelessly flux and "change."

John Adams said, "Statesmen by dear Sir, may plan and speculate for Liberty, but it is Religion and Morality alone, which can establish the Principles upon which Freedom can securely stand… The only foundation of a free Constitution, is pure Virtue, and if this cannot be inspired into our People, in a great[er] Measure, than they have it now, they may CHANGE THEIR RULERS, and the forms of Government, but they will not obtain a lasting Liberty." [my emphasis]

Most Americans still aren't buying "the death of God," but the bad news is that the elitists of the academia-media complex don't give a HOOT what you think. Alexis de Tocqueville made a prediction 170-some years ago: "The surface of American society is covered with a layer of democratic paint, but from time to time one can see the old aristocratic colours breaking through."

"Today there are more Marxists on the Harvard faculty than there are in Eastern Europe." So says George Will. I'm just reporting what he wrote, but it's probably close to being literally true. The East learned its lessons the hard way behind the Iron Curtain. Although they were founded by churches, the Ivy League schools have become the very embodiment of Anti-religion, and they are greatly imitated by people who want to be considered very "smart." However, any dumb farmer could tell you:

> "It is with man as with wheat; the light heads are erect even in the presence of Omnipotence, but the full heads bow in reverence before Him."
>
> - Cooke

Because of "Education LITE," the Great American Experiment is in for the fight of its life, a PSY-WAR of epic proportions. Social engineering is en vogue, and the social engineers are manipulating education, psychology, public relations, the media, politics, the courts, and even our language to their own personal advantage - our Judeo-Christian heritage "be damned." The motto of the National Council for the Social Sciences is, "Transforming cultures; past, present, and future." Their agenda is no longer concealed, and they certainly do twist the "past."

> "He who controls the past controls the future; he who controls the present controls the past."
>
> - George Orwell

A war of cultures is all about semantics, "spin," and rewriting the past. "He who controls words controls the source of true power," someone once said. Francis Bacon said, "It is a strange desire to seek power and to lose liberty."

The word "Freedom" is becoming passe ("past its prime") and Abraham Lincoln said, "We all declare for liberty; but in using the same word we do not all mean the same thing." Milton said: "None can love freedom heartily, but good men; the rest love not freedom but license."

Edmund Burke said, "Among people generally corrupt, liberty cannot long exist… The people never give up their liberty but under some delusion… Kings will be tyrants from policy, when subjects are rebels from principle… Learning will be cast into the mire, and trodden under the hoofs of a swinish multitude" [Students Wildly Indignant about Nearly Everything, in Al Capp's words].

> But versed in arts that, while they seem to stay
> A falling empire, hasten its decay.
>
> - William Cowper

We could learn a thing or two from the fall of the British Empire. Jefferson said, "In matters of style, swim with the current, but in matters of principle, stand like a rock"! Don't try to make too much of the fact that TJ wasn't a "joiner" of churches. As William Lamb (1779-1848) said: "While I cannot be regarded as a pillar, I must be regarded as a buttress of the church, because I support it from the outside."

"Just another lovely day in paradox?"

Liberals accuse Traditionalists of simple-mindedness, but it is they, the "avant-garde" agents of "eternal change" who are putting society, and thus even education itself, in mortal danger. Life is a great paradox, and "liberals" can't handle a paradox (and why is a funny, funny riddle). Our Alexander Hamilton (1757-1804) started writing brochures at the age of 17 and wrote for 30 years. He died in a "duel" in which he essentially committed suicide. He's another one of those men of Faith that the history revisionists somehow "can't find" - or else lie about because they simply don't agree with them. Men such as Hamilton are a "BURR" under the saddle, and he said:

> "To grant that there is a supreme intelligence who rules the world and has established laws to regulate the actions of [His] creatures; and still to assert that man, in a state of nature, may be considered as perfectly free from all restraints of law and government, appears to a common understanding altogether irreconcilable. Good and wise men, in all ages, have embraced a very dissimilar theory.
>
> "They have supposed that the deity, from the relations we stand in to himself and to each other, has constituted an eternal and immutable law, which is indispensably obligatory upon all mankind, prior to any human institution whatever. This is what is called the law of nature… Upon this law depend the natural rights of mankind."

Speaking of the "ship of state," George Bernard Shaw put it this way: "The captain is in his bunk, drinking bottled ditch-water; and the crew is gambling in the forecastle. She will strike and sink and split. Do you think that the laws of God will be suspended in favour of England because you were born in it?" (or, do you think that because YOU were born in the 'New World Order' that the Law of Nature and of Nature's God can be outlawed? I guarantee you, this world is not long for this world unless we can get our act together. The curtain is about to fall. Shaw also said:

> "Democracy substitutes election by the incompetent many for appointment by the corrupt few."
>
> "A democratic government is the only one in which those who vote for a tax can escape the obligation to pay it," said Tocqueville. Thus we "pick the pockets," don't we?

The current strategy of the elitists appears to be the lowering of education standards so that as many people as possible can be bribed with "free" handouts and other delusions. That way, the "few" get to go on appointing Federal judges and the Supreme Court Justices who will gradually stifle and outlaw REAL freedom. We have the worst of both worlds, democracy and aristocracy.

Tocqueville said: "Our contemporaries are constantly excited by two conflicting passions; they want to be led, and they wish to remain free: as they cannot destroy either one or the other of these contrary propensities, they strive to satisfy them both at once. They devise a sole, tutelary, and all-powerful form of government, but elected by the people.

"They combine the principle of centralization and that of popular sovereignty; this gives them respite: they console themselves for being in tutelage by the reflection that they have chosen their own guardians. Every man allows himself to be put in leading-strings, because he sees that it is not a person or class of persons, but the people at large that hold the end of his chain.

"After having thus successively taken each member of the community in its powerful grasp, and fashioned them at will, the supreme power then extends its arm over the whole community... such a power does not destroy, but it prevents existence; it does not tyrannize, but it compresses, enervates, extinguishes, and stupefies a people, till each nation is reduced to nothing better than a flock of timid and industrious animals, of which government is the shepherd."

Lincoln said, "If the policy of the government upon vital questions affecting the whole people is to be irrevocably fixed by decisions of the Supreme Court... the people will have ceased to be their own rulers."

John Adams said, "The moment the idea is admitted into society that property is not as sacred as the laws of God; and there is not a force of law and public justice to protect it, anarchy and tyranny commence."

Think eminent domain and "income redistribution." Not that the elitists care one whit about the "laws of God," but one-fifth of the Ten Commandments deal with the sanctity of private property, which includes your income, believe it or not. Does a "majority" have the legal right to steal it?

> "Once the public coffers of the federal government are opened to the public, there will be no shutting them again."

Those were the words of President Grover Cleveland (1885-1889), who said in his first inaugural address, "In the discharge of my official duty, I shall endeavor to be guided by a just and unstained construction of the Constitution, a careful observance of the distinction between the powers granted to the Federal Government and those reserved to the States or to the people." The three branches of the Federal Government now tend to see the Constitution as a nuisance, a road block to their agendas, rather than a road map to guide us on the only road to Freedom.

The crux of the problem:

Alexis de Tocqueville said: "I seek to trace the novel features under which despotism may appear in the world. The first thing that strikes the observation is an innumerable multitude of [lay]men [but]... Above this race of men stands an immense and tutelary power, which takes upon itself alone to secure their gratifications, and to watch over their fate...

"It would be like the authority of a parent, if, like that authority, its object was to prepare men for manhood; but it seeks on the contrary to keep them in perpetual childhood...

"[This elite class] chooses to be the sole agent and only arbiter of that happiness: it provides for their security... regulates the descent of property, and subdivides their inheritances - what remains, but to spare them all the care of thinking and all the trouble of living... [and get this] It covers the surface of society with a network of small complicated rules, minute and uniform, through which the most original minds and the most energetic characters cannot penetrate, to rise above the crowd..." [My emphasis, but if you need a translation of that, Ronald Reagan put it this way]:

> "For many years now, you and I have been shushed like children and told that there are no simple answers."

"It's all for the children," they say, but, ironically, they do not allow children to go through a "normal" childhood. Having deprived children of the right to their childhood, through "sex education," it is easy for the elite political class to keep them in "perpetual childhood" - so as to avoid dealing with the root causes of our problems, and keep people distracted from the real issues!

Tocqueville saw the beginnings of this phenomenon. He said, "In the United States, the majority [read "mainstream"] undertakes to supply a multitude of ready-made opinions for the use of individuals, who are thus relieved from the necessity of forming opinions of their own."

"He was just an actor," they said, but in actuality President Reagan was a one-man Think Tank. He went over the heads of the media and got through to the people for a change. Reagan said:

"We've been tempted to believe that society has become too complex to be managed by self-rule, that government by an elite group is superior to government for, by, and of the people. Well, if no one among us is capable of governing himself, then who among us has the capacity to govern someone else?" The Gipper was simply echoing the first inaugural address of Thomas Jefferson, who said, in the terminology of his time:

> "If there be any among us who would wish to dissolve this Union or to change its republican form, let them stand undisturbed as monuments of the safety with which error of opinion may be tolerated where reason is left free to combat it...[Should we] abandon a government which has so far kept us free and firm on the theoretic and visionary fear that this Government, the world's best hope, may [possibly lack] energy to preserve itself? I trust not.
>
> "I believe this, on the contrary, the strongest Government on earth... Sometimes it is said that man can not be trusted with the government of himself. Can he, then, be trusted with the government of others? Or have we found angels in the forms of kings to govern him? Let history answer this question... . Possessing a chosen country... acknowledging and adoring an overruling Providence, which by all its dispensation proves that

it delights in the happiness of man here and his greater happiness hereafter - with all these blessings, what more in necessary to make us a happy and a prosperous people?

"Still one thing more, fellow-citizens - a wise and frugal Government, which shall restrain men from injuring one another, shall leave them otherwise free to regulate their own pursuits of industry and improvement, and shall not take from the mouth of labor the bread it has earned."

Those timeless words don't need translation, but one little aside here: Deists don't talk about "blessings" or an "overruling Providence," but our post-modern educators, being 180-degrees off from the "patron saint of the 'Democratic' party," twist some of Jefferson's words from his youth and portray him - and most of the Founding Fathers - as "deists" (or worse) and they never quote Jefferson's later words! History revisionism is a matter of "selective reporting" in the spirit of the prevailing "news" media.

John Eidsmoe writes, "The colonists were familiar with deist thinking. But deism never gained a strong foothold in America. The first Great Awakening, the religious revival of the 1740s, was partially responsible for cutting short the spread of deism." To paraphrase another thing he said, the Constitution "can buy time for a nation" (during times of "flux") until cultural stability can be reestablished. James Madison said:

"If the sense in which the Constitution was accepted and ratified by the Nation... be not the guide in expounding it, there can be no security for a faithful exercise of its powers." Jefferson said:

"The Constitution on which our Union rests, shall be administered by me according to the safe and honest meaning contemplated by the plain understanding of the people of the United States at the time of its adoption." And Justice Felix Frankfurter declared [my emphasis]:

"What governs is the Constitution, and not what we have written about it."

As Lincoln, and Rush Limbaugh, have said, "Words mean things," or at least they did. In the New Age of "enlightenment," the "Queen's English" is being trumped by the "Queen of Hearts" (i.e., words mean "what we want them to mean," emotionally). All is flux and "change." We think we are "up to date."

"The intellectual life is about your feelings," said Susan Sontag, a revered modern nerd (I used to never use that word, but now I figure let them know how it feels when they put down us rednecks and "dumm Kopfs" outside of higher education who attempt to defend our Roots).

"Who can refute a sneer?"

- William Paley (1743-1805)

The elitists in education have nothing but a sneer for all of the principles, values, and beliefs held dear by our national - and spiritual - "Fathers." Deviancy isn't the only thing they're defining down; they're redefining what "America" means, and my first "word-for-the-day," boys and girls, is "sabotage" (as in sabotaging the American Revolution). Can you say "sabotage"?

In the original sense of the word, the root for sabotage meant "to clog" or "to clatter along," as if wearing clogs or "thongs." Thus a scouting party could be "sabotaged" by the noise of a scout's feet - just as national security can be undercut by giving our enemies false perceptions of the American people (as nothing but quitters, perverts, corrupt, and no longer religious).

Excuse me? Despite a few "flip-flops," there is still a "Majority of faith" out here in the Outback, "fly-over country," or Backwater USA. Just as "thongs" are no longer worn on the feet though, patriotism is no longer worn on our shirt sleeves (at least that's the perception). In spite of the WTC 9-11 attack, the secular liberals figure that they can still eliminate patriotism and other "vestiges" of Traditionalism, "given enough time." Seventy years of "reeducation" in Russia wasn't enough time (I have a 1917 Wisconsin license plate that survived in a roadside ditch longer than the Evil Empire lasted).

The only "conspiracy" I believe for certain is the conspiracy of the Educrats. This time they intend to be more "systematic." The hippies who decried the "Establishment" 40 years ago tell us that we can stop questioning Authority now, because they are the Authority. Incrementalism or creeping socialism is much like the man who cut off his dog's tail one inch at a time on the theory that it wouldn't hurt so much.

General MacArthur said, "I am concerned for the security of our great nation; not so much because of any threat from without, but because of the insidious forces working from within."

> "The world doesn't owe you a living. It was here first."
>
> - Mark Twain

Ever since the "kings" of this chosen country started assuming the role of "angels," or benefactors made in the image of the social engineers - ala Santa Claus - the threats to our borders and our culture have become as serious as the threat to our language and our sovereignty! And in the words of one former Presidential candidate, "The government breaks your leg and then offers you a crutch." Anyone who thinks that the government won't mess up health care and everything else just doesn't know his history.

> "I see it is impossible for the King to have things done as cheap as other men."
>
> - Samuel Pepys (1633-1703)

As government grows, the culture goes to pot. "Envy never takes a holiday," said Bacon, and neither does the demagoguery of journalists and opportunistic politicians who literally hope for the worst! Can it get any sicker than that? Actually yes, things will probably get worse before they get better.

"Massey-Harris 101"

"Sickness, symptoms, and root causes":

This will sound "overly-simplistic" to our over-specialized academics, but any farmer could tell you that we reap what we sow, and I was in fact a farmer first. One of our Presidential hopefuls said that he/she can't see what was so good about the "olden days," but I think that the county I used to live in got through the 1950s without one murder.

The county's "Human Services" department consisted of the sheriff and one volunteer named Pop Wendt who worked with a handful of juvenile delinquents. Private charity and families took care of the charity needs. Today the Human Services department has its own multi-million dollar court house annex, and there are more social problems and crime than ever before. While the Left frets about "trans-fats," fast food, and offensive speech, about 17,000 Americans suffer every year from drug overdoses, and thousands die from drug-related shootings. And they die young! What is wrong with this picture?

Right now, cities such as Ben Franklin's "City of Brotherly Love" are averaging more than one murder per day - while the guides at Independence Hall expunge all references to the religion of the Founding Fathers from their "lectures," not unlike our college and university professors - even while our politicians invite more and more gang-bangers across the border and throw Border Patrol agents into solitary confinement for doing their job too well - while "pardoning" White House turkeys at Thanksgiving and drug dealers at Christmastime.

As Jenkin Lloyd-Jones used to say, "Have we reached the stomach-turning point yet?"

In German lingo, "Vas is los," or, have we gone stark-raving mad?

Casey Stengel once said, "I don't like them fellas that drive in two runs and let in three." Not to name names, but there are certain sentences that should never be completed:

- America has been good to us, but -
- Public education could be improved, but -
- This time we're really really serious about securing the borders, but -
- Thanks for the history lesson, but -

In this book, you will be treated to a smorgasbord of great quotes from my columns - which I like to call "60-second Seminars." One of the main themes of my column is that it's high time for "Generation XYZ" to read the actual words of our Founders (who appealed to "the Supreme Judge of the world for the rectitude of their intentions" in the Declaration of Independence)! The Founding Families were overwhelmingly religious families, and they didn't raise "no fools."

> "So much of left-wing thought is a kind of playing with fire by people who don't even know that fire is hot."
>
> - George Orwell

Ironically, the Left looks upon most "religious" people as CULT members, even while peddling the "Cult of Hope." The Left is not only trying to sell us snake-oil; they're trying to get us to buy the whole snake. One of the little-known facts is that cult, cultivate, and culture all came from the same root word. The original meaning of the root word was "to move around, turn," and it came to mean "to be busy, inhabiting a place, or making a wild place suitable for crops" (as in the sense of "turning the soil"). Interestingly, that root word also came to mean "to worship," while the Latin version of "cult," colere, gave us the word "COLONY." [Ayto's "Dictionary of Word Origins"]

Translation: The upshot of all this is that the 13 American colonies were essentially "cults" - inhabited by farmers who were "busy" worshiping, "turning" the soil, and making this a "suitable place" to live, plus they had had to "move around" a bit to get here (some of them from England to Holland to the New World), and so they were in a sense cultists, and they could have died were it not for their Faith.

I might add that the Puritans and Pilgrims often compared themselves to the Israelites coming out of Egypt into the Promised Land, and the term "Christian" was first used as an epithet meaning a "cult." By the way, "to be busy" could also refer to good BUSI-ness people. No bum ever fed a hungry child, but businesses do! No bum ever offered you a job, did he?

A very wise man I once met used to say that as long as 51 percent of the American people keep on trying to do the right thing (regardless of their brand of religion), God's hand would continue to be "over," and protecting, us. Sadly, America is turning into a "wild place" again.

Our homogenized population seldom talks about "achievement," and some people abhor it. "Hero," like cult, has become a 4-letter word. The heroes of the American Revolution are castigated whenever they can't be totally ignored. History is history! It has been turned over like bread dough and mingled with the leaven of "social science," which is 95 percent "art" and five percent "science" - but no history!

The cunning connivers of history revisionism started out sounding "innocent" enough: "George Washington never cut down a cherry tree"; Daniel Boone "never wore a coonskin cap; it was beaver." This would be innocuous in and of itself, but when they start saying that Jefferson and most of the Founders were "deists," and Abraham Lincoln may have been a homosexual, it becomes obvious that there was a pre-existing "agenda" there.

They might as well come right out and say it: "If Washington had cut down a cherry tree, he probably would have lied about it to his father" (Washington probably cut down a LOT of cherry trees in his life, but there is NO evidence that he was a liar). I hate to have to point out the obvious, but the Educrats just don't want American children to have any heroes (except perhaps the Educrats themselves). "They're saving the planet, you know," he said sarcastically.

"When men were men, women were women, and schools taught":

Yes, the Good Old Days got more things right than "Zeitgeist 2000" does. I used to think that the agenda of the public schools was well-intentioned but just misguided. I have decided that I was being too kind. They know what they're doing, and they're doing it on purpose! At any rate, it is inarguable that the Founders are being slandered in the schools. Washington's name has even been removed from some school buildings, and "Founding Fathers" is a no-no term, thanks to the radical feminists.

Speaking of spiritual analogies, the Great American "experiment" was like the baby Moses floating on the water. Talk about miracles – Moses "walked on the water" before being able to walk - but anyway, the Founding Fathers witnessed a lot of miracles, and all they could do was give this chosen country a shove in the right direction. They knew that they wouldn't always be around to "mother" us. And as of late, the "mainstream elites" are only taking us "down the river," back to slavery.

> "It is a dangerous thing when we too easily accept new ideas as truth... Man's memory is short. The very generation which God freed from Egypt turned to grumbling within one month after their liberation. Their eyes were on the fleshpots of Egypt."
>
> - The Rebirth of America
> (DeMoss Foundation)

Yes, murmuring and complaining appear to be genetic with us, and so is loss of memory and the pull of the flesh. We taxpayers are even going to build a "memorial" to the Woodstock "Festival." That's tantamount to the building of the Golden Calf by those complainers of old in honor of their orgy at the foot of Mt. Sinai. This "ain't" a good sign. I'm afraid we'll "pay" for that in more ways than one!

> "Remorse, the fatal egg by pleasure laid."
>
> - William Cowper

Throughout recorded history, the worst examples of slavery always occurred under godless or pagan regimes. If the Founders were realists about one thing, it was about human nature. That's why they spent so much time trying to put checks and balances on positions of power in government, and why John Adams said that the Constitution was "made for a religious people."

By using Freedom against Freedom, the secularists may yet drive religion underground, as "back in the good ol' USSR," and they may yet achieve their "secular society" - for a while - but it would never last. "A house divided cannot stand," I think someone said.

When Mitt Romney mentioned Adams in a major speech, the pretty young things reading the "news" almost went "like eeeww!" They acted as this were the first time they had ever heard of a John Adams. On second thought, maybe it was! Our learned "commentators" told us that John Adams was all wet, even as families in Omaha were planning funerals for their dead loved ones shot in a mall. Just when we had almost forgotten Columbine too, mall shootings and school shootings are becoming a fad again. But we like to forget.

> [Sidebar: It's curious to note that the Salt Lake City mall shooting occurred on the eve of the announcement of the candidacy of a Mormon for President (and the shooter was given a hero's burial in Bosnia). Also, the Omaha mall shooting occurred about the same time as his speech on religion and the Founding Fathers.]

Even as more believers were being shot in Colorado, the mainstream media were mounting their horses and shouting, "The theocrats are coming; the theocrats are coming." One could write a poem about it: "The Midnight Ride of the Religophobes" ("one if by the Internet; two if by talk radio"). And the issue of "the rule of Law versus the rule of Personality" wasn't even mentioned in the "Presidential debates." Explaining his comment about the Constitution being "for a religious people," John Adams said:

"There must be a positive passion for the public good, the public interest, [and] honour... established in the minds of the people, or there can be no republican government, nor any real liberty: and this public passion must be superiour to all private passions." Adams not only said that our Constitution was made for a religious people, but that "it is wholly inadequate for the government of any other"!

Tocqueville said, "The best laws cannot make a constitution work in spite of morals... That is a commonplace truth, but one to which my studies are always bringing me back."

Just before the "Roaring 20s," President Wilson said that "in every generation all sorts of speculation and thinking tend to fall under the formula of one dominant thought of the age. For example, after the Newtonian Theory of the Universe had developed, almost all thinking tended to express itself in the analogies of the Newtonian Theory and since the Darwinian Theory has reigned amongst us, everybody is likely to express whatever he wishes to expound in terms of development and accommodation to environment." The winds of "change" were blowing.

"Enter the followers of Freud, stage left":

Speaking of passion and playing with fire, the disciples of Freud wrote that in order to change the traditional political beliefs into a controllable "consensus," there had to be a Sexual Revolution in America [Wilhelm Reich, 1929]. Our farm boys got to see 'Paree' during WWII, so Freud's disciples were sure that they would never go back to those old "country" values.

After Alfred Kinsey's coming, our modern academics started complaining about "sexual repression" in the 1950s, as if the slightest amount of "guilt" were the worst thing that a human being could possibly experience. After Hugh Hefner came along, they were sure that the time was ripe for the "final stage of societal evolution."

The "Youth Revolution" of the 1960s was no accident. It was planned. The hippies, not trusting anyone (except their college professors) over the age of 30 - - thought that they had stumbled onto an entirely new concept - except that there's nothing new under the sun. Unbeknownst to them, they were nothing more than copycats of the 1860s Nihilists in Russia (who assassinated a Czar in 1881 and "pioneered" the Bolshevik Revolution of 1917).

President Reagan was shot 100 years to the month from the assassination of the Czar. There was no "glory" in Woodstock or the Youth Revolution. It was simply a copy-cat crime by useful idiots, and the bottom line is that history didn't begin with the trendy zeitgeist of the NINETEEN sixties! And those who cannot see very far into the past cannot see very far into the future either (to paraphrase someone). Do you really think that we are escaping the fate so many other nations suffered? Please note that it took about 50 years for the radical socialist movement in Russia to be sown, sprouted, cultivated, watered, established, and detasseled (by internal purges). There were only crop failures in the end.

If history does repeat, our time of grace may be just about "up"; it has been about 50 years. We promised to never invade Cuba, and "watched" the fall of Venezuela, where rights watchers are now being assassinated. Has anyone out there ever heard of the Monroe Doctrine? Probably not many anymore, but incidentally:

Despite the popular media P.R. blitzes during the 60s, most kids didn't protest. Most people didn't buy the Playboy philosophy either, and even today, more high school kids have not had sex than have had. Teenagers today are actually more pro-life than they were 10 or 20 years ago. Despite the lefty sermons on "relativism," and zero-tolerance for dissent, most people still don't want a mate who is "relatively faithful" (Zig Ziglar says).

Of particular "concern" to Academia today is the failure of the American people to totally buy their psycho-babble on the subject of the Origin of life. Darwinism is the rock-bed foundation of their dearest dogmas such as purposelessness and sexual "freedom." One of the more honest evolutionists, Aldous Huxley, openly admitted that escape from traditional morality was the main goal for him and his friends.

So where are we really, "at this point in time"?

The summer 2006 issue of On Wisconsin reported that "A recent survey by the Pew Forum on Religion and Public Life found that three-fourths of Americans are dissatisfied with Darwin's explanation of life. A Gallop poll last fall reached a similar conclusion, adding that a majority of the dissatisfied were educated men and women - in fact college graduates… and of those who did accept evolution, most considered the process so complex as to need the help from 'an intelligent designer.'"

The author of the article tried to be "balanced," but the premise of almost everyone she talked to on campus was: "We must figure out a more effective way to package and sell Darwinism (because it's the truth and we're the most highly evolved people since time began)." I'm reading between the lines, but that, essentially, is their unstated doctrine.

George Orwell said, "There are some ideas so wrong that only a very intelligent person could believe in them."

"Dogmas always die of dogmatism."

- Anais Nin

Darwin's faithful are the most dangerous "cultists." Thomas Moore (1779-1852) said, "But faith, fanatic faith, once wedded fast to some dear falsehood, hugs it to the last." [For more, read:

"Evolution: The Thalidomide of Social Silver Bullets" - www.RenewAmerica.us/columns/dahlgren/031020]

As I said, the bad news is that the "tutelary powers," including the "Big Box" universities, don't care what you think! A paleontologist said, "In China we can criticize Darwin, but not the government. In America, you can criticize the government, but not Darwin."

In Canada, the Law says that even home-schooled children must be indoctrinated with the theory of Evolution – a law which crushes the whole idea of home-schooling (and Freedom).

Thomas Jefferson would be shocked. He actually spoke out against the old Greek fables of evolution that were being recycled in Merry Old England in the 1700s by Charles Darwin's grandfather. Jefferson admitted that "few in their after years have occasion to revise their college opinions," but he would be simply amazed to learn that "errors of opinion" can no longer be FREELY opposed "with reason and truth" - or even "dumb questions"!

The Left decries "divisiveness," and bemoans the freedom of "US versus THEM" - because THEY are essentially monopolists in spirit, which is the spirit "by which despotism arises in the world."

> "There is a Northwest Passage to the intellectual world."
>
> - Laurence Stern (1713-1768)

David Horowitz said, "Politics is a choice of comrades… My personal odyssey has given me much less respect for intellectuals. I respect street smarts." I would call it "horse sense," but if you get the point, that was coming from an intellectual himself.

In actuality then, this isn't a "you and me against the intellectuals" book; it's our intellectuals against their intellectuals - because "our" intellectuals really understand theirs!

President Reagan said that a Communist is someone who reads Karl Marx, but an anti-Communist is someone who understands Marx. And as Groucho Marx said, "A child of five could understand this. Someone go fetch a child of five."

Karl Marx wanted to dedicate Das Kapital to Charles Darwin, and though Darwin declined, his "ideas" had far-reaching consequences. When he wrote the Communist Manifesto, Marx assumed that the capitalist system in England had reached maturity, and had failed. This was sophistry. In reality, economics was a discipline still in its infancy, and so, with faulty premises, Marx came to faulty conclusions! And real people suffered horrible tragedies that were anything but "abstract"!

We owe a lot to the graduates of our engineering schools, and the other "hard sciences," but it is the "soft sciences" that have hijacked the schools of Education, the "front offices," and Boards of Regents of our colleges and universities in the name of "political correctness." In Josh Billings' "Encyclopedia of Wit and Wisdom" (1874), Henry Wheeler Shaw said, "The trouble with people is not that they don't know but that they know so much that ain't so."

Given their "modern" philosophies, which they try to pass off as "mainstream," Liberty is now thought to mean the right to do anything and everything we WANT to do, not the right "to do what we ought" (in the words of Lord Acton, whose words would be called "superstition" and "hate speech" now).

WELL (as Reagan might say), in the words of George Orwell, "If liberty means anything at all, it means the right to tell people what they don't want to hear."

By the way, an intellectual opponent once said of Tocqueville that he had begun to "think" before he began to "learn." In other words, the "mainstream" educators didn't get TO him soon enough, and therefore they lost "control" of him (there was no Federalized "day care," and it takes a "village" to brainwash a child, you know). BTW, I share my birthday with Tocqueville and Dag Hammarskjold (July 29th). Though U.N. Secretary-General Hammarskjold died in a suspicious plane crash years ago, his book "Markings" is still in the book stores. He wrote:

> "The longest journey is the journey inward… The more faithfully you listen to the voices within you, the better you will hear what is sounding outside… There is a point at which everything becomes simple and there is no longer any question of choice, because all you have staked will be lost if you look back. Life's point of no return…

> "I believe that we should die with decency so that at least decency will survive... I don't know Who - or what - put the question; I don't know when it was put. I don't even remember answering. But at some moment I did answer Yes to Someone - or Something - and from that hour I was certain that existence is meaningful and that, therefore, my life, in self-surrender, had a goal..."

No, I don't have a "sheep" skin yet, but I'm not complaining, because my life has a goal, and as Mark Twain said, "I never let schooling interfere with my education."

As one of my favorite writers, Ferrar Fenton, said: "I was in ['53] a young student in a course of study for an entirely literary career, but with a wider basis of study than is usual... Indeed, I hold my commercial experience to have been my most important field of education, divinely prepared to fit me [for my life's work], for it taught me what men are and upon what motives they act, and by what influences they are controlled.

> "Had I, on the other hand, lived the life of a Collegiate Professor, shut up in the narrow walls of a library, I consider that I should have had my knowledge of mankind so confined to glancing through a 'peep-hole' as to make me totally unfit... "

As my biography at RenewAmerica.us says: "Curtis is listed as a University of Wisconsin-Madison "alumnus" (loosely speaking, along with a few other dropouts including John Muir, Charles Lindbergh, Frank Lloyd Wright, and Dick Cheney)." James Lovell is another "dropout" who went on to the Naval Academy and the moon, but Lindbergh is the only one mentioned here who "flunked out" of the UW.

"Truth or consequences":

The coin of the realm, liberty, has two "flip" sides. For every right there is a responsibility. There is no excuse for irresponsibility in a nation that has a Heritage as rich as ours. "Academic freedom" gives no one the "right" to turn our nation's history on its head. Nor does freedom of the press, when the media are flippant with the facts. Pop-culture, Academia, the media, and the State have become intellectually incestuous, and a Traditionalist doesn't have much chance of breaking into the "loop." That's not news, but sometimes it can be an advantage.

"I can think outside the box, because I'm not IN the box," says Michael Savage.

Let's "think outside the boxer shorts." Today's educators and "journalists" (and some politicians) are so shallow that they can't even see their own self-contradictions - or as they would say - "cognitive dissonance." By the forcing of Groupthink, they have no more use for the "politics" of the much-cited Martin Luther King, Jr. - or even Jackie Robinson's - than they have for real men of dissent such as Clarence Thomas, Bill Cosby, Thomas Sowell, or an Alan Keyes (who like Lincoln lost a bid for the Senate from Illinois).

The seeds of our "wild oats" have gone to weeds and all those "weeds" have borne the bad fruits of ignorance and anarchy, unto the third and fourth generations. The latest grisly murders are so common that they're generally reported on page three, under "News in brief." We're starting to get used to it. One of the popular catchwords of the social engineers is "well-adjusted" (which really means "sheep-like"). The corollary is, anyone who thinks that we are reaping what we sowed – and complains - just isn't "well-adjusted." I submit that we are becoming a bit TOO well-adjusted. If you're "well-adjusted" in a world as wacky as this one, you must be totally whacked out.

"Why are the hyenas laughing?":

History doesn't repeat itself exactly all the time, but nothing that does happen should ever surprise us anymore, because there's a cause for every effect. Regarding the "New Thought" philosophies of the late 1800s that laid the groundwork for Freudianism [and hedonism], in Charlie Sykes wrote, in "A Nation of Victims" (1992):

"The results were not what the prophets of liberation had envisioned... Instead of being freed from the oppressive bonds of the past, [man] found himself alone in a world without mooring, norms, sense of direction, or purpose."

The sanctity of human life has been devalued by "the spirit of the Age," and I know whereof I speak, because I've lost eight close friends to murder. This book is dedicated as much to them as to you my readers, "so many of whom [to borrow a phrase] belong to the human race."

That's not funny, because even the "hard sciences" are coming to the point where the idiots are talking about implanting artificial intelligence into human beings, building robots with a sense of emotion, and even making love to robots. Hard to believe almost, but my dad was born before the Wright brothers got their airplane off the ground. Almost as amazing as how much science has changed is how fast it has changed. I can remember hearing my first sonic boom, but the latest supersonic jet will be able to fly half way around the world in five hours.

"Many shall run to and fro, and knowledge shall be increased."

- Daniel (534 B.C.)

Did you know that one can even get a degree in the philosophy of "Futurism"? The University of Houston offers one. "On Wisconsin," the alumni magazine (winter 2007), published an article in which some "futurists" are quoted. Niki Dennison wrote:

"In a time of tumultuous change, when we can't possibly keep up, [David Zach] advises that we have to 'figure out the things that don't change - and when you find those, it gives you a place to stand.' Not all change is progress, he says, and 'sometimes the most radical thing to do is to not change'... [and he] believes that we need to pay more attention to history, community, and families.'

"He describes his favorite futurist as G.K. Chesterton, because he believes that Chesterton embodies something that we are short of in our modern era: the willingness to learn from the past. 'The more things change,' Zach says, 'the more we must learn from the past. We live in an age where anything is possible, but that's scary, because not all things should be possible.'

"Chesterton advocated, he says, 'giving votes to our ancestors'."

I was just shocked to read this in a publication from the University of Wisconsin! Surprahse, surprahse! "The democracy of the dead"! But if I may quote further, the article concludes:

"'We assume that today is the most important thing and dismiss the past, blaming the past. History is full of accomplishments, and we should have gratitude for them. We have temporal arrogance.'

"And finally, although we may be opening a Pandora's box of nanotechnology, genetics, and robotics, Zach points out that the last thing in Pandora's box was hope. 'You must have hope,' he says. 'It's a moral imperative.'" [my emphasis]

WOW! I don't know how many UW students these days could define "temporal" to save their lives - or their eternities - but AMEN (with that one disclaimer: "Hope makes a good breakfast, but it is a bad supper"). Although I repeat myself, Bacon said that, and I hope that I don't have to explain the meaning of that! "Hope" has its limitations, you know.

Jim Lileks of the Minneapolis Star-Tribune wonders if America isn't already into "the Wile E. Coyote mode" - beyond the edge of the cliff, but just not yet into the free-fall. I submit that we may be heading for hell without a hand-basket to our name. Red ink in the Federal budget is like "no problem," while teachers worry about hurting the feelings of students by grading papers with red ink. Go figure, eh?

The Conclusion of the matter:
No more bull!

Abraham Lincoln said, "We shall meanly lose or nobly save this last hope on earth."

In my first book, I said, "So often these days we are told that, in the minds of the elite speakers, this or that issue has become so difficult, so COMPLEX, that the rest of us will simply have to agree with them and forgo all attempts to rectify the situation." BULL-loney! We've wasted too much time already. Dr. Arthur Voobis, writing for the Estonian Theological Society in Exile wrote:

"It is not my place as an historian to play the part of a prophet. Nevertheless, I am convinced that if we are not willing and ready to live up to the facts, we shall perish in our incurable ignorance and stupidity. We have little, very little time to awaken the minds and hearts of people to the present fateful reality. In confronting perilous times, we must do all we can to take the Christian responsibility more seriously than ever before...

> "Indeed, all of what we observe in the mirror of recent history about political leadership recalls day-flies warming themselves in the autumnal sunshine without an inkling of the fact that winter is coming."

It's time for books to speak "plainly" rather than in abrstractions! "Matters of fact... are stubborn things," said Matthew Tindal (1657-1733).

"Whenever a man talks loudly against religion, always suspect that it is not his reason, but his passions which have gotten the better of his creed," said Laurence Sterne (about a century before Darwin wrote his "thesis")!

Aldous Huxley's exact quote was: "The reason we accepted Darwinism even without proof is because we didn't want God to interfere with our sexual mores."

Curtis Dahlgren

"What is truth, said jesting Pilate; and would not stay for an answer."

- Francis Bacon

"Las trahison des clercs ('the treason of the educated classes.'"

- Julien Benda (1868-)

I think he was paraphrasing P.T. Barnum (who may have said), "There's a sucker born every minute." And that's why the hyenas are laughing!

However, as Boris Pasternak said, "In every generation there has to be some fool who will speak the truth as he sees it."

By the way, the 1950s-style atmosphere up here in the "frozen tundra" has made me even more determined to complete this project, and Siberia, in a sense, seems to have had the same effect on many Russian intellectuals (the good ones), though the 1950s were for them hardly "Happy Days." In the words of William Shakespeare, I sit down to write this book with "a countenance more in sorrow than in anger."

America is still such a young country that only 74 years (one lifespan) separated the deaths of Thomas Jefferson and John Adams, on the 50th anniversary of the signing of the Declaration of Independence, from the birth of my father! America is too young to die.

Have you ever prayed that God won't have to "destroy America to save America" from even further cultural degeneration? There may be some people who can't wait for it to happen, so their "predictions" will come true, but I'm not that way! Every day I'm praying for one extra day of Freedom and one less day of tribulation.

Abraham Lincoln said that the philosophy in the classroom today will be the philosophy of government tomorrow. You can also get a clue as to the state of your future "New World Order" from the ethics of the medical profession and Nazi-style medical experiments being performed by "scientists" (human embryo cloning, for example). Whittaker Chambers said:

> "Man without God is a beast, and never more beastly than when he is most intelligent about his beastliness."
>
> "Learning is like mercury; one of the most powerful and excellent things in the world in skillful hands; in the unskillful, the most mischievous."
>
> - Pope

In "The German Euthanasia Program, Excerpts from 'A Sign for Cain,'" Dr. Fredric Wertham said that "when Hitler was just starting his career, the 'life devoid of value' slogan was launched from a different source. Evidently there is such a thing as a spirit of the times which emanates from the depths of economic-historical processes." He was referring to the "interruption" of life philosophies being promoted in the universities in Leipzig, etc., in the 1920s by legal and medical "experts."

I don't care if you have 10 PhD degrees; if you say a foolish thing, it's still a foolish thing. Our "cutting-edge" technological ethics and hip culture these days had many parallels in both Russia and Germany in the days just preceding the times of greatest tragedy for those nations. How can we expect to escape the same fate when we are cloning human embryos?

There's a debate going on in Traditionalist camps between the optimists and the pessimists. It's sort of like a good-cop, bad-cop scene in a movie, and the jury is still out on which side is right. The optimists admit that we may be on thin ice, but the pessimists can't even see the ice.

Never mind "Conventional Wisdom": The case for restoring Traditional Values:

My, my! This "brief Introduction" turned out to be about as "brief" as a "Philadelphia lawyer's" briefs, so pretend that you're a Judge making a monumental decision, and your decision will determine what kind of a People, what kind of a Nation - and a World - we will become. It literally might, and I hope that you do not overlook the obvious: we do have a CHOICE. Leo Tolstoy said:

> "There are two methods of human activity... there are two kinds of people: one use their reason to learn what is good and what is bad and they act according to this knowledge; the other act as they want to and then they use their reason to prove that that which they did was good and that which they didn't do was bad."

The Old Testament prophets would be able to relate to that. Of all the signs of the times, none is more frightening that the extent to which cultural values we traditionally perceived as good are - as predicted - currently condemned as "hatred," "intolerance," "out of date," and "cliched." Well, I for one am sick and tired of having my grandmother (the one I knew) being labeled a "religious extremist" or a "fundamentalist fanatic."

We have been "shushed like children" and told that there are no simple answers, but it's not all that complicated. We have been told since the Garden of Eden to "choose life." Maybe Thomas Jefferson was a "fundamentalist extremist" too? For example, in his second inaugural address, he said [with my emphasis]:

"I shall need, too, the favor of that Being in whose hands we are, who led our fathers, as Israel of old, from their native land and planted them in a country flowing with all the necessaries and comforts of life; Who has covered our infancy with His providence and our riper years with His wisdom and power, and to whose goodness I ask you to join in supplications with me that He will so enlighten the minds of your servants, guide their councils, and prosper their measures that whatsoever they do shall result in your good, and shall secure to you the peace, friendship, and [approval] of all nations."

P.S. Just a few words more:

Even if you are a "believer" or a recovering liberal, I may have some things to say that even YOU "won't want to hear." The secular and the "progressives," who don't want to be "labeled," want you to just shut up, you know. They say, "Can't we all just get along (and shut up)?" But we're not all "going in the same direction," are we?

If you are young, your public school is teaching you to blend in rather than to "stand out." If you are in college, you have been conditioned NOT to talk about "religion and politics" in public, even while "they" continue to do so (speaking mainly negatively about the former). And the churches are being much too easily muzzled by the IRS, and the ACLU - which operates with impunity and immunity (and on the taxpayer's dime).

THIS MUST END; THE "SILENT MAJORITY" HAS BEEN TOO SILENT, TOO LONG.

John Keats said, "For the sake of a few fine [imaginative]… passages, are we to be bullied into a certain philosophy engendered in the whims of an egotist[?]" And Edmund Burke said:

> "When bad men combine, the good must associate; else they will fall, one by one, an unpitied sacrifice in a contemptible struggle."

Do those words sound "too political" for you? Do you say, "I don't want to get involved"? If you've read this far, you must have at least some interest in history, so why not "politics"? To put it simply:

> "History is past politics, and politics present history."
> - Sir John Robert Seeley (1834-1895)

Whether you like it or not, there is an "us versus them" tug-of-war going on for the hearts and minds of the American, and Western, world. So let's take stock of what we're up against: On their side they have Darwin, Kinsey, and Kevorkian - one of whom married his cousin, one who had an unusual obsession with pedophilia, and one who was an example of a death-wish, simply a clumsy forerunner of what's in your future.

On "my" side we have Bacon, Burke, and Blackstone, Washington, Adams, and Jefferson; Tocqueville, Solzhenitsyn, Pasternak, and Orwell, et al; Lincoln, Reagan, Thatcher, and King David, who said, "Who are these Philistines who have defied the God of Israel?" In other words, "We win. They lose."

We also have hundreds of believing scientists on our side, from Pasteur to Einstein to von Braun - plus the original Designer and Logos, who said:

> "You are the salt of the earth, [but] if the salt has lost its savor, how can it be salted? It is then good for nothing, but to be tossed out, and trodden under the foot of men."

Of certain professing Christians, He said, "I have 'somewhat' against you."

They were "lukewarm, and the only way that evil can triumph over good is by its becoming the default position - by forfeit - by your NOT EVEN SHOWING UP IN THE ARENA OF IDEAS! You may be a little "square" - like salt is - but if you never get out of the salt shaker - your inner circle of friends - "what good are you?" I'm talking about "Christians" who are a bit, "somewhat," too smug!

Casey Stengel said, "If we're going to win the pennant, we're going to have to start thinking we're not as good as we think we are."

> [Translation: "Apathy, self-righteousness, and overconfidence can become the biggest enemy of confidence itself."]

Yogi Berra said, "Theoretically there isn't much difference between theory and practice, but in practice, there is."

Translation: "Perception isn't always reality, and unless you walk the walk as well as 'talk the talk,' we get the kind of education and government we deserve in the end."

Where else but here are you going to be able to go from Casey to Yogi to Huxley (sounds like a new double play combination; Huxley is Chance); Thomas Huxley said that the great tragedy of Science was "the slaying of a beautiful hypothesis [faith] by an ugly fact [evolution]."

That's the story they're sticking to and the translation is, his comrades are SERIOUS about "slaying" your faith, and maybe you! A Darwinist recently wrote to a church publication, "Only when religious extremists such as you are wiped from the face of the earth will mankind be free of the hatred, stupidity [etc]... You are as bad as child molesters, spewing this nonsense to impressionable young minds. Thoughtful, rational people can only hope your kind will die off quickly, while there's still time for reason & sanity to save this planet from idiots like you."

"Save the planet." Keep that phrase in mind. When Christians and other practicing believers are persecuted and killed, which happens every day, the optimists may expect to be killed by a fanatic (secular or otherwise), but the pessimists may be expecting to be killed by a "thoughtful, rational person who is just trying to save the planet." [A little sarcasm there.]

> "Man is a creature who lives not upon bread alone, but principally by catchwords."
>
> - Robert Louis Stevenson (1850-1894)

Of course, when I, as a Traditionalist, make a statement that makes sense to too many people, the post-modernists will say that I am "dealing in cliches." But someone once said: "Abundant use does not automatically make a saying trite or a fairy tale (if so, Darwinism's 'settled truth' and 'indebatable facts' would have become a hackneyed cliche long ago)."

Aristotle said that "man is by nature a political animal," and sadly, education has become a very political animal. And since Christians are the (perceived) enemy of those who dominate "higher education," the latter have made the enemy of their enemy, radical Islam, their (perceived) "friend." You can try to "take the religion out of politics," but you can't "take the politics out of religion." The Archbishop of Canterbury now advocates Sharia Law for Muslims in Britain.

A very wise man I once met used to say that it is a lot harder to UN-learn something than to learn the Truth in the first place. How true, and it is also a lot harder to learn it the hard way, if you know what I mean.

> "Just because you do not take an interest in politics does not mean that politics will not take an interest in you."
>
> - Pericles (Athenian statesman, 490-429 B.C.)

Rudyard Kipling said:

> If you can keep your head when all about you
> Are losing theirs and blaming it on you...
> If you can wait and not be tired of waiting,
> Or being lied about, don't deal in lies,
> Or being hated, don't give way to hating,
> And yet don't look too good, nor talk too wise;
> If you can dream - and not make dreams your master;
> If you can think - and not make thoughts your aim;
> If you can meet Triumph and Disaster
> And treat those two imposters just the same...
> If you can walk with crowds and keep your virtue,
> Or walk with Kings - nor lose the common touch,
> If neither foes nor loving friends can hurt you,
> If all men count with you, but none too much;
> If you can fill the unforgiving minute
> With sixty seconds' worth of distance run,
> Yours is the Earth and everything in it,
> And - which is more - you'll be a Man, my son!

[For those unaccustomed to classical literature, that doesn't translate well into modern lingo, but here's an approximation: "It's YOUR head - so use it or lose it - whether you're female, male, or whatever!" In other words, "WAKE UP and LOOK UP."]

The moderns just hate Rudyard (the-tail-must-wag-the-dog) Kipling (1865-1936). Regarding elitism-over-people, one of those other old English writers wrote earlier even:

> Ill fares the land, to hast'ning ills a prey,
> Where wealth accumulates, and men decay;
> Princes and lords may flourish, or may fade;
> A breath can make them as a breath has made;
> But a bold peasantry, their country's pride,
> When once destroy'd, can never be supplied...
>
> - Oliver Goldsmith (1728-1774)

"A mind quite vacant is a mind distress'd," said Cowper (referring to the small and great alike).

"We are all in the gutter, but some of us are looking at the stars."
- Oscar Wilde

America, Please Look Up And Phone Home!

PPS: The lack of footnotes in this book was intentional. I didn't want anything to interrupt the word flow but, in a general way, I will credit my sources in the Appendix. The quotes are all verifiable ones, so if you want footnotes, you can do your own! We have bigger problems to worry about right now than footnotes or "carbon footprints." The immediate "State of the Union" is not good at all.

President Kennedy warned us NOT to ask what your country can do for you, remember? Now we constantly ask what the country can do for us. But have you ever asked what you can really "do" for your country? If you seriously wanted to do something, remember: one of the best things you can "do" is turn off your stupid television and read a BOOK! Horace Mann once placed an ad in his newspaper that said:

> "Lost somewhere between sunrise and sunset, two golden hours, each set with sixty diamond minutes. No reward is offered, for they are gone forever."

If you give this book a few minutes a day, the following sections will provide more details of the general premises that this overview laid out, and will give you some clues as to what you, as an individual, can "do for your country."

> There up spoke a brisk little somebody,
> Critic and whippersnapper, in a rage...
>
> - Robert Browning (1812-1889)

Chapter 1
- The Traditional family vs. "Popular" culture -

("TRICKLE-DOWN TRASH")

Introduction: "The Philistines, the Populace, and the Jezebels"

"There is a strange indifference which characterizes modern [society]. Nevertheless, those who have lived through the inferno of Bolshevist rule and have seen its unmasked face and learned its real aims feel that something must be said. They would speak even if their word of warning find little attention in this time when the hearts of men are peculiarly and quickly seized by prattle which comes upon them from every side."

- Dr. Arthur Voobis

"But that vast portion, lastly, of the working-class which... is now issuing from its hiding-place to assert an Englishman's heaven-born privilege of doing as he likes, and is beginning to perplex us by marching where it likes, meeting where it likes, bawling what it likes, breaking what it likes - to this vast residuum we may with great propriety give the name of Populace. Thus we have got three distinct terms, Barbarians, Philistines, Populace, to denote roughly the three great classes into which our society is divided."

- Matthew Arnold (1822-1888)

Here's what the Encyclopaedia Britannica, 11th edition (1910), has to say about the 1860s hippies in Russia (who were identified in a book entitled Fathers and Children in 1862):

"Thanks to Turgeniev, these young persons came to be known in common parlance as Nihilists, though they never ceased to protest against the term as a calumnious nickname. According to their own account, they were simply earnest students who desired reasonable reforms, and the peculiarities in their appearance and manner arose simply from an excusable neglect of trivialities in view of graver interests... the males allowing the hair to grow long and the female adepts cutting it short, and adding sometimes the additional badge of blue spectacles...

"Their appearance, manners and conversation were apt to shock ordinary people, but to this they were profoundly indifferent, for they had raised themselves above the level of so-called public opinion, and despised Philistine respectability...

"For aesthetic culture, sentimentalism, and refinement of every kind they had a profound and undisguised contempt [and]... rather liked to scandalize people still under the influence of what they considered antiquated prejudices...

"With the impulsiveness of youth and the recklessness of inexperience, the students went in this direction much farther than their elders, and their reforming zeal naturally took an academic, pseudo-scientific form.

"Having learned the rudiments of positivism, they conceived the idea that Russia had outlived the religious and metaphysical stages of human development, and was ready to enter on the positivist stage. She ought, therefore, to throw aside all religious and metaphysical conceptions, and to regulate her intellectual, social and political life by the pure light of natural science.

"Among the antiquated institutions which had to be abolished as obstructions to real progress, were religion, family life, [and] private property... Religion was to be replaced by the exact sciences, family life by free love, private property by collectivism..

"Some of the Nihilists maintained that things were not yet ripe for a rising of the masses, that [peaceful] propaganda must be continued for a considerable time, and that before attempting to overthrow the existing social organization some idea should be formed as to the order of things which should take its place. The majority, however, were too impatient for action to listen to such counsels of prudence, and when they [such as Tkachev] encountered opposition on the part of the government they urged the necessity of retaliating by acts of terrorism...

"In accordance with the fashionable doctrine of evolution, the reconstruction of society on the tabula rosa might be left, it was thought, to the spontaneous action of natural forces, or, to use a Baconian phrase, to natura naturans." [emphasis mine]

"All great change in America begins at the dinner table."

- Ronald Reagan

In 1908, a family went to church together. The preacher held up the Bible and pounded the pulpit, and everyone was very quiet on the way home. As they ate dinner together, no one had to ask what the preacher was "trying to say," because they all understood!

In 1958, a couple dropped off their kids at church, and went to play golf. Later they asked the kids what the preacher had talked about. "Sin," was the reply. "He's against it."

In 2008, a latch-key kid went to church with a buddy and when he got home, his mother asked him what the preacher had talked about. "Hatred," was the reply. "She's against it."

"She just hates it," said the kid, as he pounded the dinner table with his fist.

"Anything else?" asked his mother.

"Yeah, she says it takes a village to raise a child," says the kid, pounding the table.

"Why are you hitting the table with your fist?" asks his mother.

And the kid says, "Because I'd sure like to know what village my dad lives in."

"Whatever," said his mother, as she opened a government check.

Section 1A:
"A conversation with Gramma Greenberg"
www.RenewAmerica.us/
columns/dahlgren/060421

That a lie which is all a lie may be met and fought with outright,
But a lie which is part a truth is a harder matter to fight.

- Alfred, Lord Tennyson (The Grandmother)

[I HAD A DREAM.] Hi Gramma! Sorry I missed your funeral. I think it was a school day.

Oh, I didn't notice. Dead people are, well, dead, you know. But what's new?

Well, I hardly know where to start, but for one thing, people like you used to be called the pillars of society. You are now called "right-wing fundamentalist extremists."

What'd I ever do to deserve that?

Easy. You had 13 kids and were a stay-at-home mom.

> With 13 kids it's hard to do anything else. What was I supposed to do - walk the streets?

You were supposed to get a job.

> For Pete's sake, washing clothes alone took us from sunup to sundown. But tell me more.

Well, we now have same-sex marriages you know.

> Who has the kids?

The right-wing fundamentalist extremists.

> You mean "Christians?"

Exactly. Hollywood still makes some movies to remind us of the olden days, but that reminds me - there is now more material in a pair of boys basketball pants than in the high school girls' dresses. 'Course they don't wear those much anymore.

> What do they wear?

Levis.

> Farmers' pants?

Yes. They even wear Levis to church. 'Course not many go to church anymore. Maybe just to get married or something.

> Are you kidding me?

I wouldn't kid you, Gramma. 'Course marriage isn't very fashionable anyway. In some cities, 90 percent of the kids are born out of wedlock, and two-thirds of those kids never make it through high school.

Some of my kids had to drop out of high school too, but they were all productive American citizens.

That's right, and those 13 kids produced approximately 55 productive American citizens. But don't get me started on the subject of citizenship!

WHY?

Well, now you don't have to be an American citizen to get federal aid.

What's that?

Money from the federal government to get such things as free food and education, even college for non-citizens.

Who's running this country now anyway?

Lawyers.

Figures. I sure hope none of my descendants are lawyers.

Not a single one. You taught the Greenbergs how to fight their own battles. You always gave us good advice such as: "Thank the Lord for small favors" and "'Every little bit helps," said the mosquito when he peed in the ocean." Of course that was before ecology and sociology.

What's THAT?

That's one of the "backbones" of Higher Education now. Essentially, it's a class in learning how to sue people who "offend" you.

So what else is new?

Well, remember how you used to tell your kids, "That problem will go away when you get married"? Nowadays it's so hard to find a dependable mate, that half of the marriages end in divorce. Even the marriages of some of your own grandchildren.

"Massey-Harris 101"

    I don't want to hear about it.

Wait'll I tell you about the public schools. The kids can hardly read, but they get "A"s in sex education.

    WHAT?

Yes. They teach it in elementary school now. And some of the teachers do hands-on teaching of sex education. And you don't need to know how to read your diploma to get one.

    Do those kids become right-wing fundamentalist extremists?

No, they become totally dependent upon politicians, and vote - nine times out of ten - to continue the present course of education and government. And did I mention the Mexican border?

    No, why?

Well, 2 or 3 million people, we call them Hispanics now, walk into California, Arizona, New Mexico, and Texas every year and demand their Constitutional rights, hire lawyers, and fly Mexican flags at protest rallies.

    What are they protesting?

They're protesting the American taxpayer. For trying to slow down the invasion.

    I'm getting a headache, and you know I had a bad heart. I think
    I want to go back to sleep.

Wait. Let me tell you, some public schools have banned T-shirts with the American flag on them, and some community associations have banned the flying of the American flag.

    What flag do they fly?

Some cities fly "Homosexual Pride Parade" flags - with words printed in both English and Spanish.

[sigh] What else is new?

Well, the courts are trying to ban the Pledge of Allegiance, and "In God We Trust" from our dollar bills. And some people are filing lawsuits to silence church bells, because they they are really "ticked off" by them.

Stop, stop!

But there's more - the New York Times and other newspapers are taking the side of the lawyers who want to silence the church bells and keep God and the Founding Fathers out of the public schools.

They can't do that.

They think they can do a lot of things. 'Course their subscription lists are dwindling every day.

How do people get the news?

On our laptops.

I don't even want to go there.

Computers. We have these tiny machines now that can send words, sounds, color photographs, and even little movies to our friends over a telephone wire. Or sometimes through the air.

Curt, I hope your problem goes away when you get married.

No, I'm serious. I don't even buy a newspaper anymore, and I threw my television set into the dumpster.

I don't know what that is, but before I go back to sleep, is there any good news at all?

Well, our passenger planes don't have propellers on them anymore, and man flew over the moon and landed on it.

> You're such a kidder. Now I know you're making up this whole story. Glory be.

Wait'll I tell you what's going on in the Middle East.

> Not one word, or I'll have to wash your mouth out with soap. The next thing is, you'll be trying to tell me that we're giving the Holy Land to the Philistines.

We've already succeeded in giving them most of it. The State Department now tries to stay neutral except when it can give land to the Philistines, or independence to Islamic provinces of Christian nations.

> I SAID HUSH!

It's been nice seeing you, Gramma. I'll talk to you again in a few, after the Lord has straightened out this whole mess. Oh, by the way, you'd better stop encouraging mosquitoes to pee in the ocean. That could get you arrested for "hate speech" and "environmental crimes."

> FIDDLESTICKS! I suppose you're going to tell me that it's even illegal to spank a naughty child!

Well DUH. Of course!

> That'll be the day, when I die again! [she muttered to herself]

[As Gramma wandered off to look for a bar of soap and a paddle, I woke up on the couch and turned off the TV.]

Section 1B:
"Can you say 'JADED,' boys and girls?"
www.RenewAmerica.us/
columns/dahlgren/031104

Curtis Dahlgren

"The superior man knows what is right. The inferior man knows what sells. Now if we could only figure out how to do both."

- old Chinese proverb, paraphrased

I LIKE OLDE ENGLISH, because originally the word "prude" was never applied to men - and it was the highest compliment one could pay a female. The word "prudefemme" in Old French meant (literally!) "a fine thing of a woman." "Preu" meant "fine," "brave," "virtuous" and it gave the English the word "proud" - which is also an okay word in the best sense of the word. We could use some old-fashioned pride, instead of phony "self-esteem."

This is certainly not the topic I wanted to cover today, but I happened to read the 10/28/03 USA Today. A sidebar on page one got my attention: STRIPPING GOES MAINSTREAM:

"Strip clubs aren't just dives frequented by men... Other than demand for dollar bills, what does it mean?"

Never mind the California fires story, I said to myself, this could be BIG! So there was the story about an Atlanta nightclub:

"STRIPPING'S NEW SIDE: DANCERS BUMP STEREO-TYPES, GRIND INTO MAINSTREAM."

"As a dozen naked women undulate on three stages, Susan ------ fires up a cigar and leans back in one of the leather armchairs... The 48-year-old and a quartet of pals are in TGIF mode. 'Yea for the fact that women can walk into a strip bar without an escort,' [her friend exclaims]."

You can almost hear the writer, Kitty Bean Yancey, going "Yea! Yea! Yea!" And the phrase "Just report the news; don't encourage it!" came to mind. Immediately below that story was another one on L.A.'s "Fashion Week," LaLa Land's answer to New York City's. A fashion analyst said:

"It's all very competitive. It isn't just about the clothes coming down the runway. It's this morphing of a world - it's sexy and visible, and a lot of people have decided, 'I want to get in.'"

I'm sure the promoters of L.A. Fashion Week were jealous of all the ink the fires were getting in the L.A. Times, but there is something to this morphing of a world. Something strange has happened to all of us. I've noticed that people of both genders can now walk past "sexy and visible" naked women at the checkout-counter without giving them a second glance. And since when is this a good thing?

Proverbs 31's "pearl-of-great-price" has become a pig-in-a-poke. NO WONDER this country has to spend millions on a "little blue pill"!

When I am confronted by ladies or school girls in public who are less than fully dressed, I am tempted. I am tempted to ask them, "Do you really think I'm so stupid that I wouldn't be able to determine your sex unless you exposed yourself? Or is it that you think your face is so ugly that I wouldn't know your gender unless you showed them to me? Which is it?"

Just as there's a time to laugh and a time to mourn, there's a time and place for that stuff, but I deeply resent being forced against my will to look at them in public. I've been aware that women have two and cows have four ever since I was old enough to walk, so you don't have to prove it to me. And don't turn around and call me a "prude" or a dirty old man. You don't have to say, "You don't have to look." I say that some people aren't "oversexed" - they're just under-brained. Gramma Greenberg would say that modern fashions are the height of "discourteousness."

According to my trusty '38 Funk & Wagnalls, the word "jaded" doesn't refer to the stone by that name but to an older noun meaning (1) "an overworked, worn-out horse" or "a sorry nag"! The second-choice definition is "a low, worthless person, specifically a vicious woman; wench; hussy"! Hearts of stone are involved, though (and they're not diamonds or rubies).

Curtis Dahlgren

According to the 1973 Miriam-Webster Dictionary of Synonyms, the verb to "jade" means to "tire, weary, fag, or tucker," and analogous words include satiated and emasculated (i.e., "sick of" or, "having a belly-full")!

Yes, the pop-culture fads and fashions are just another form of control-and-castration of men, and the only place the "mainstream" can take you is down the river. It's a paradox and very few "get it."

P.S. Hollywood's charge that the liberation of Iraq is the one thing that made the Arabs hate us is as hilarious as the Playboy "discovery" of sex. Islam doesn't hate us because we are "too religious" or too "fundamentalist"; it hates us because we are (post-Christian) "paganists" - the very thing that Hollywood applauds and awards! Talk about "The Ugly American," Hollywood's "beautiful people" aren't.

Immediately after the liberation of Iraq, an Iraqi theater owner started showing American XXX movies. This may have won him some friends among his patrons and the western media, but it certainly makes the job of our military personnel awkward and deadly. For many reasons, but for this reason alone, America needs a spiritual reawakening.

I used to work with a Mohammed who was born in the jungles of Indonesia, and he once said to me, "America is evil, isn't it?" He was married to a Jehovah's Witness, so he wasn't referring to religion. He was referring to our pop-culture. He also had some strange conspiracy threories about the WTC attack which I can't agree with (the only conspiracy theory I accept for sure is the one against the American Family by the education Establishment and by the media), but the least you could do is:

Turn off that stupid TV!

Section 1C:
"As long as no one gets hurt,
what's the big deal?"
www.RenewAmerica.us/
columns/dahlgren/040229

"Shoot to Live!"

- the Weathermen

"Until you're prepared to kill your parents, you're not really prepared to change the country because our parents are our first oppressors... American youth is looking for a reason to die."

- Jerry Rubin

"A revolution is not a dinner party, or writing an essay, or painting a picture, or doing embroidery."

- Mao Tse-tung

"The time is right. Eat leaden death, Imperialistic reactionary business administration majors."

- "SDS," Vol. 1, no. 2
(Students for a "Democratic" Society, 1969)

[The following piece is one that I wrote shortly after the Janet Jackson "half-time show" at the Super Bowl in 2004, and just before the release of "The Passion of the Christ."]

SPEAKING OF "TIMING," IS IT A COINCIDENCE that the Super Bowl "half-time show" and the gay "weddings" all happened just before the opening of "The Passion of the Christ"? Is it yet another "coincidence" that LaLa Land will shower "awards" on the films that would never win "hearts and minds" in Iraq?

In the 1960s, America was in denial about a "revolution," and in the 1990s we were in denial about a Culture War. Today we are in denial that this Culture War is one with international consequences. An ordinary citizen from Wyoming said it best in a letter to CBS about the Super Bowl "show." Among other things, he said,

> What really bothers me is that, after reading all of the news stories, I find that CBS still doesn't realize what they did, and why it was wrong. Well CBS - here is why: American soldiers are engaged in a culture war in Iraq and Afghanistan. At this point in the battle, it's no longer our armies against their armies; it's our ideas of freedom and liberty against the enemy's ideas of fear and repression. America has put out a message of hope to the world - live free, have hope, and enjoy the fruits of a free and open... society. The Super Bowl half-time show poisoned that message...
> [end excerpt]

It's not my job to comment on the decision to go to Afghanistan or Iraq, but once America (and Britain) went, let's not forget that our holy book says, "When you go to war against your enemies, keep you from every evil way." The Iraqi people must be wondering how we can straighten out their mess if we don't even follow our own beliefs. Those who ask "What's the big deal?" about the popular culture, sadly, wouldn't know a "big deal" if it clobbered them upside the head. In 2004, the mayor of San Francisco decided to promote "gay marriages" contrary to a law specifically voted into law by California voters. Will this backfire? Gay marriages wouldn't fly in Iraq, you know.

Do not take these issues lightly. At Gettysburg, Lincoln said, "We are now engaged in a great Civil War, testing whether this nation or any nation so conceived and so dedicated can long endure." At the Harvard Law School Forum in 1999, Charlton Heston said:

> "Those words are true again. I believe that we are again engaged in a great civil war, a cultural war that's about to hijack your birthright to think and say what resides in your heart... I serve as a moving target for the media who've called me everything from 'ridiculous' and 'duped' to a 'brain-injured, senile, crazy old man.'"

Hollywood hated the release of "The Passion of the Christ" at just about the time of "Academy Awards" week. And never mind Mel Gibson - it wasn't about him. It was essentially about the cost of redeeming our sorry S&H green stamps! It's also about rulers in high places in this world and the role of the common people - as in "Do NOT give us Barabbas." Americans and Brits will have similar choices to make in the days ahead.

In The Religion of Abraham Lincoln (1963), William Wolf says:

> The Puritan heritage distilled through the 18th century patriots without, however, loss of its original religious strength explains many features in Lincoln's thought. It is the background for the predestinating will of God, for corporate and individual responsibility, for the direction of democracy as a way, for America as 'God's almost chosen people,' for belief in the wisdom of the people, for the possibility of making a solemn vow and covenant with God and observing its historical results, for the importance of 'discerning the signs of the times... ' His political action, as revealed by his own words, was ultimately the social expression of an understanding of God and of man that demanded responsible activity. This is contrary to a widespread modern opinion that religion should be a separate interest or even a hobby in life...

That latter opinion sums up our zeitgeist, the spirit of the age. People in education and the media believe that going to church is almost but not quite on a par with going to the gym or "going" to the bathroom (perhaps "harmless"). And Flip Wilson's "Church of What's Happening Now" has become a reality. Both pundits and churchmen are repulsed by the "Old" Time Religion, and "True Believers" are considered "unfit" to hold the office once held by the Great Emancipator (sounds kinda "judgmental," doesn't it?).

"Tolerance" is going to be the death of us. Every time a Traditionalist speaks up, he is accused of "judging" and being a "hypocrite." Dumb question: "But isn't that JUDGING?" I don't know why, but the question occurs to me, what would be my parting advice should I never write anything again? For some reason, the line that comes to mind is one of Yogi Berra's:

"When you come to a fork in the road, take it."

I'm not "selling" anything. I wouldn't try to sell you my religion, nor Mel Gibson's, and if you're turned off by "organized" religion, you could always start a disorganized one. I'm being mostly facetious here, but not entirely (your "salvation" is none of my business, but right now I'm more concerned about the survival of the nation).

"A pox on red necks and white collars?":

By the way, I don't know why the Lefties are so upset with "white collar crimes" these days. They're the ones who tried to tell us that "there are no moral absolutes," "if it feels good, do it," and "the only eternal verity is CHANGE." The white collar criminals may have "followed suit," but the moral relativists are the ones who LED that suit, and leading with your strongest trump card can backfire!

In the February 13, 1997 Hagar the Horrible strip, his sidekick Lucky Eddie says, "Hagar, explain to me again the 'Viking theory of economics.'" Hagar says:

> "Well, some people have too much stuff. It's the Viking's job to relieve them of some of their stuff so it gets spread around."

Eddie says, "What if they come and take their stuff back?" and Hagar says:

> "Now you're talking about STEALING!"

On February 20, 2008, Hagar the Horrible did an encore of his 1997 strip. Hagar is sitting at a bar in England and says to the guy next to him, "What do you do for a living?" The guy says:

"My name is Robin Hood! I rob the rich and give to the poor!" Hagar says:

"How can you live if you give all the money to the poor?" And the guy says:

"I DIDN'T SAY I GIVE IT ALL TO THE POOR!" [thanks, Chris Browne]

Comedian Dick Gregory said, "The NAACP is a wonderful organization. Belong to it myself. But do you realize if tomorrow morning we had complete integration, all them cats would be outta work?"

There must be a lesson in there someplace for preachers of the popular "social gospel." Christ said that when you help the poor, "Do not sound a trumpet before you, as the hypocrites do in the synagogues and in the streets [as on a political soapbox with a megaphone]." Don't you dare call it "family values" when you "soak" the rich and give half of it to the poor (and unqualified) whom you refuse to teach economics. Christ said that we would always have the poor among us (and obviously the "rich"), and he wasn't "above" being buried in a rich man's tomb.

Bottom line: If you really want to "help the poor," stop punishing achievers. Slicing up a finite pie will leave us ALL poor, but a growing pie and the "multiplier effect" produced by achievers keeps money in circulation. Big corporations aren't your biggest enemy. You can only skin a sheep once.

Grampa Dahlgren used to say, "Thank God for the rich people; the poor people don't have any money." He used to farm 500 acres with horses and peddled the milk door-to-door in town. He gave a lot of milk to poor people who couldn't pay their bill, but he broke even because of the people who could! I think that's why he was so vehement about the evils of socialism. Alexis de Tocqueville said:

> "Democracy and socialism have nothing in common but one word, equality. But notice the difference: while democracy seeks equality in liberty, socialism seeks equality in restraint and servitude."

There's a big difference between "inequality" and "inequity." Christ never taught "From each according to his ability, to each according to his needs" (SHOW ME the chapter and verse). What He did preach was the wisdom of acquiring at least enough so that, if you have kids, you can leave something behind for them when you die, and while you're alive, "Provide."

The "excess profits" RED herring:

Here's Economics 101 in one sentence: (a) If I were to get one penny from every person in the United States, I would be a millionaire three times over! I would have "excess profits," but this could be either good or bad, depending on whether my method was legal or illegal; (b) no penniless school dropout "ever fed a hungry child" or offered your family a job; some work is required; (c) work makes money and money makes work (the more people who are qualified to work, the more money made).

"So many people in the wagon; so few people pulling the wagon," I believe Phil Gramm said. Too many people don't seem to understand that those "free federal dollars" were our dollars in the first place. Hubert Humphrey admitted as much when he once said:

> "O, my friend, it's not what they take away from you that counts - it's what you do with what you have left."

Be careful what you wish for if you wish you could steal Bill Gates' money. Even Woodrow Wilson understood: "The history of liberty is a history of limitations on governmental power, not the increase of it. When we resist, therefore, the concentration of power, we are resisting the powers of death, because the concentration of power is what always precedes the destruction of human liberties."

But enough said of this socio-economic morality debate! Before "situation ethics" and the "Youth Revolution," traditional parents simply taught us the value of self-reliance, telling the truth, taking responsibilities as seriously as "rights," and exercising individual initiative. That's why they called the 1950s the "Happy Days."

P.S. [To summarize this section and to bring it "up-to-date"]:

I bought the 12/18/07 USA Today. I don't watch TV and don't buy many newspapers, but they ran a story with a headline above the center fold, "This time, 'family values' are lower on the agenda." The subhead was, "Shift reflects rise of 'weighty' issues - and a changing America."

They were referring to the Presidential primaries, and the obvious insinuation is that "family values" are "SO yesterday." The gist of the story is about some USA TODAY/Gallop poll that claims that American voters have "grown" and have moved "beyond" such issues as abortion, gay marriage, and the brainwashing of our children in the public schools on sex (my words).

[Isn't it interesting that no major newspaper has ever run an above-the-centerfold story about polls that show that 3/4 of the American people are dissatisfied with Darwin's explanation of the "Origin" of life on earth? And no newspaper has ever published an above-the-centerfold poll showing that religious people experience more satisfying sex than the non-religious?]

Anyway, the story said, "The 'traditional' family - a married couple with kids - made up fewer than 22% of U.S. households last year, according to the Census, down from 40% in 1970... [depending how you define 'household']. Nearly two in five U.S. births last year were out of wedlock, more than twice as high as in 1980."

By reading between the lines, the "message" for politicians is, "You'd better shut up about traditional family values if you want to get anywhere in politics these days." And sure enough, the politicians in Washington fear the Post more than they fear their own constituents back home. The New York Times will applaud any politician who stifles the people, and it has a fit if anyone prints the Truth. And polls have been known to lie "from time to time."

> "There is no such thing as a New York intellectual establishment. It just looks that way from the outside."
>
> - Jason Epstein
> (former editor-in-chief of Random House)

Curtis Dahlgren

Leaving aside the question as to the "winning strategy" for the politicians, a more pregnant question would be: "Given our crime rate and other social problems (and the 'brilliance' of the social engineers), then what has society been doing wrong since 1970?" Could it be our focus? Have men been neutered? Have women given up their moral high ground? Or what?

Here are some quotes from Times columnist Maureen Dowd [my emphasis]:

> "Even as a child, I could feel the rush of JFK's presidency racing forward, opening up a thrilling world of possibilities and modernity... Our first lady was setting the pace in style and culture...[But in the 2000s] We're entering another dark age, more creationist than cutting edge... [which is] happy to crush the liberal ELITES inspired by Kennedy's New Frontier under the steamroller of 19th-century family values."

"Yeah, right." By definition, the very thing that makes liberalism elitism is the fact that most of the country isn't "WITH IT" out there "on the cutting edge," of course. There is a critical intersection of culture, education, economy, and politics - especially when the will of the people is defied the way it is being defied right now by the cultural powers-that-be. As for those "possibilities" promised by the self-described "liberal elites," let's be perfectly clear:

> "To believe only possibilities, is not faith, but mere Philosophy."
> - Sir Thomas Browne (1605-1682)

So much for "inside the Beltway," on the East coast, but let's not forget the Left. Here are some pithy quotations from LaLaLand about those who worship modern "style and culture":

> "Hollywood's a place where they'll pay you a thousand dollars for a kiss, and fifty cents for your soul."
> - Marilyn Monroe

"Hollywood is like an empty waste basket."
- Ginger Rogers

"Hollywood is one big whore."
- Freddie Prinze

"They have great respect for the dead in Hollywood, but none for the living."
- Errol Flynn

"I would not willingly eat anything that had intelligent life. But I would willingly eat a producer."
- Marty Feldman

"Trash seeks its own level."
- Celeste Huston

"Success means never having to admit you're unhappy."
- Robert Evans

"If you ask me to play myself, I will not know what to do. I do not know who or what I am."
- Peter Sellers

"I've never been out of this country but I've been to California. Does that count?"

- Bob Bergland
(former Secretary of Agriculture)

Curtis Dahlgren

PPS: "Conclusion America: This is an S.O.S. for the American family, Titanic-style!"

I have just been reminded of the fact that the good ship Californian was only 20 miles from the Titanic when it struck that iceberg, but when the S.O.S. went out, the radio operator on the Californian was SLEEPING. This is SO typical!

The good ship "State-of-California" is becoming nothing more than a Lollipop. The Ninth circus Court of Appeals is trying to torpedo America, while the Hollywood liberals shake, rattle, and roll in their mansions in Beverly Hills and Malibu. I love mansions, have worked on trees at "many mansions" - so some of my best friends are mansions – but Hollywood calls us "hypocrites" for daring to speak up for "19th century family values." As for hypocrisy, what have they done with money they had left? And "had" is the operative word there, given the state of the economy as I write.

According to the story, Samuel Johnson was being taken on a tour of the estate of the famous English actor, David Garrick, and after viewing the mansion and the grounds, Johnson shook his head and said, "Ah, David, David, these are the things that make the deathbed terrible!"

One of the producers of a famous sit-com said, "There are a lot of empty cemeteries out there, and when they are filled, the world will be a lot more tolerant place." A sword that swings both ways!

> "God loves all men, but He's enchanted by none."
>
> - author unknown

Michael Savage says that we need an uprising against the popular culture by those Traditional women of America who are "so 19th century" (Dowd's words, not his). Is that "trying to turn back the clock"? No one's trying to do that. The sixth column I ever wrote was on that subject: [www.RenewAmerica.us/columns/dahlgren/031009]

I said that turning back the clock is a must when daylight savings time ends. No one is saying "go back to the 19th century" (or the 7th), but there are things we can learn from the past. I said, "By doing the right thing at the right time you can avoid the need for grief counselors in the school later!" But by refusing to learn from the past, our liberal friends aren't "moving the hands forward"; they're taking us into a wormhole, a Black Hole.

It's 20-to-12. It's time for a Cultural counter-revolution, a New American Revolution. The time is ripe for that "steamroller of 19th-century values." Resistance to resistance is futile! Ironically, one of the best quotations on the subject of Family came from Marilyn Monroe:

> "I don't mind living in a man's world as long as I can be a woman in it."

It's impossible to add much to a statement such as that - except for "viva la difference."

Oh, and - the last man to leave California, please turn off the TV.

Section 1D:
"A Time to Laugh and a Time to Weep"
www.RenewAmerica.us/
columns/dahlgren/031003

> "Anger is better than laughter."
>   - Ecclesiastes [Olde English version]

MICHAEL SAVAGE made a great point on his year-end show for 2007; to paraphrase it, he said that we've been hornswoggled by the elite Left into thinking that anger and hatred are the same thing. Those who have told us this are very cunning, because now they get to tell us which things to be angry about. Being angry at THEM is "no fair," of course! That's "hatred."

No, anger and hatred are NOT the same thing. The word anger is related to "sorrow" more than to "hatred." I wrote a column about that and I'm leading off with that column here. After a friend of my neighbor read chapter one of my first book, he said, "That guy hates everybody, doesn't he?" For people not used to PLAIN writing, this time I want to give high priority to the following:

IF VINCE LOMBARDI were coaching in this day and age, he would probably be ordered to attend "anger management" classes. People today are taught to blend in rather than to stand out, and any expression of passion is considered not Psychologically Cool. Those people who don't "blend in" and who complain about attacks on their cultural roots are considered "not well-adjusted," and Lombardi wouldn't adjust well at all to the concept of "parity" or "outcome-based football" or "all competition is evil."

I used the term get "mad" in my last column without apology, even though a former President was lecturing California citizens that "whom the gods wish to destroy they first make angry." I don't know who writes his stuff, but he echoes the sentiments of academia and the news media. The 1994 elections were called a temper tantrum by "angry white males." Peaceful pro-life demonstrators are considered angry rednecks (even when they are physically attacked by "rational" employees of abortion "clinics").

WELL (as the Gipper might say) - that's weird, because I can remember the sixties when the SDS was rioting and university buildings were being blown up by fertilizer bombs, and the news media didn't call them "angry white males" - they were called "idealists."

Leaving aside the double-standard issue, what's the truth about anger? The other day, I was reading the King James version of Ecclesiastes when I made a new discovery: The KJV says, "Sorrow is better than laughter," but the inspired Hebrew word for sorrow is the same one translated as "anger" a few verses later ("Be not hasty to be angry")!

This will raise eyebrows in the psychological community, and I wish I could say I've known this for years, but the hard fact is that the English words for "sorrow" and "anger" overlap because originally they meant the very same thing! Matter of fact, the Greek, Latin, French, and Old Norse words for "anger" and "anguish" also came from the same root words that literally mean "strangled" or "constricted" (our English "angina" comes from the same root words).

In other words, as the "Dictionary of Word Origins" by John Ayto says, the original notion of "anger" was "afflicted," and "rage" didn't enter the picture until the 13th century. The bottom line is that those who "sigh and cry" over the secularization of society are afflicted by a sense of "indignation" that is justified. There is more "sorrow" than "anger" in the passion of a Traditionalist - and more anger than sorrow in the passion of a liberal.

By the way, another interesting word related to "anger" and anguish is agony. John Ayto says that its ultimate source is the Greek verb agein [as in the Aegaen Sea] meaning "to lead," and the related noun agon meant "a bringing of people together to compete for a prize," hence, contest, conflict. As it turns out though, competition and conflict is not all bad.

From "agon" was derived agonia (mental struggle, anguish), which passed into English as 'agony,' but the sense of physical suffering didn't evolve until the 17th century. The bottom line being: There can be an up side to anger, anguish, and agony - when properly used.

"The pioneers take the arrows" and "the battle of the sexes":

When Jacob wrestled with God, he wasn't condemned for competition. God admired his perseverance. There was real "agony" involved in the efforts of the Pilgrims, Mountain Men, and pioneers "to lead" the way for those of us who followed. They actually shortened their lifespans in most cases by leaving the Old Country or the East to pursue the path that they chose. Just as Jacob (or "Israel") was given a blessing, we have reaped the blessings of the agony of the Pioneers (I'm not rambling here; this is all related).

Many of the pioneers lived in tiny hamlets, but virtually all of them found spouses faithful for a lifetime. Do you think that they were all 100 percent compatible? I doubt it, but their common faiths prevailed 99 percent of the time. Today it's off to the court of divorce at the drop of a hat. Some people spend $100,000 on a wedding, but one can start a divorce for about ten bucks. Something's wrong here.

"Perseverance is willing to be unhappy for awhile," someone said. My parents were married over 50 years, perhaps as much because of "trials" as in spite of them. Not that they weren't happy, but an occasional "venting" in my family was never called "hostility." It was just "intense communication."

Yes, Michael Savage is right when he says anger and hatred aren't the same thing. Men have been had. We have been neutered by the belief that showing any intensity even a little bit is "psychological abuse." Women have been brainwashed into feeling like "martyrs" every time a man makes a counter-point (like they say, if a man talks to himself in the forest and his wife doesn't hear him, will he still be wrong?).

Life is a paradox, and the first clue to solving this puzzle was when I found out that there's an overlap between "anger," sorrow, and agony - or "a bringing of people together to compete for a prize." God is still in control.

P.S. Remember, "iron sharpens iron." Men and women are brought together to sort of compete, but not against one another. That's why I'm calling all Traditional women to a New American Revolution.

PPS: One of my early columns was entitled "Trials: Castor oil for the Soul." Here's an excerpt. www.RenewAmerica.us/columns/dahlgren/040330

> "I CAN'T WAIT for the general Resurrection (Revelation 20:5). I have 100,000 questions for Charles Darwin. Like did the means of sexual reproduction gradually evolve (maybe TOO "gradually")? When the first woman who had evolved the means

of sexual reproduction met the first man who had evolved the means of sexual reproduction, did she tell him to go lose himself in the jungle? One can see how this process could have taken "billions and billions of years!"

I jest, but maybe it was just one woman who started yelling, "Stand on your hind legs like a man, sit up straight, stop dragging your knuckles on the ground, and keep your elbows off the table!" Seriously though, as long as the female of the species essentially had her head screwed on straight, there was some "hope" for the future!

Radical feminism and the pop culture have "changed" all that. The male of the species has allowed himself to be cowed into submission, to the detriment of the female. Yes, men of intensity such as Vince Lombardi would be sent to "anger management," and Woody Hayes would be put in the loony bin. Hayes once said:

> "Anyone who will tear down sports will tear down America. Sports and religion have made America what it is today."

That was years ago, and the proverbial "Rachel, weeping for her children" would probably be locked up and put on psychotropic drugs now! Instead of that, we need a counter-revolution by the majority of women. It's time to get "MAD." Unless the Packers are on, it's even okay with me if they start yelling:

> "Turn off that stupid TV!"

Section 1E:
"Calling all Traditional women"
www.RenewAmerica.us/
columns/dahlgren/060210

When the Hymalayan peasant meets the he-bear in his pride,
He shouts to scare the monster, who will often turn aside.
But the she-bear thus accosted rends the peasant tooth and nail
For the female of the species is more deadly than the male.

- Rudyard Kipling

THE LATE WILLIAM F. BUCKLEY, Jr. wrote a column ("McCarthy had nothing on academic world," 9/9/91) in which he quoted the following from a Brown University catalog description of a class entitled "The Remasculinization of America." (they're against it, of course):

"Reaganism and masculinity go together. In this course we will examine the relationships between popular conceptions of masculinity and [take a breath] neo-conservatism in order to assess and critique the importance of gender difference in contemporary culture [take a breath]. We will draw heavily on feminist theory and cultural studies in order to consider masculinity in the context of ongoing social inequalities." [Fainting to the floor]

Buckley wrote: "If that course were the subject of 15 minutes of fun on 'Late Night With David Letterman,' all would be right in this world. But it and a thousand similarly chaotic exercises are being taught in contemporary America... If you read about such things in National Lampoon, we'd be a healthier nation. Instead, we talk about the awful things McCarthy did to the academic world in the 1950s such as what?"

Some 600 colleges and universities scheduled "The Vagina Monologues" for the school year 2006-07, and we're supposed to take them SERIOUSLY? What is wrong with this picture? Where is the "social equality" in that picture?

LET'S GET SERIOUS: It's no wonder America is falling behind other nations in math and science: about 60 percent of our college graduates each year are female, and the predominance of women in post-graduate enrollments is rising. As more and more young boys are put on Ritalin, the percentage of males in higher education shrinks. What's wrong with that picture? Do "real women" stand by and continue to allow their boys to be essentially castrated?

The fact that Brown University is fighting the "remasculinization of America" makes it pretty obvious that Academia has been promoting the "DE-masculinization of America." NO WONDER the red-blooded boys are avoiding "Higher Education" like the bubonic plague.

The ideal male-female relationship that Ron and Nancy Reagan exhibited was very "troubling" to the social engineers, and one of my first columns was entitled "Dedicated to Dutch; the reasons they hate Reagan." www.RenewAmerica.us/columns/dahlgren/031027

[Note: That column was written because a major TV network was planning to air a "docudrama" that portrayed Nancy and Ron (already failing in health) as a "dysfunctional family." Thank God that he had Alzheimer's and thus didn't have to even be "aware" of the late 1990s, or September 11, 2001.]

Can you picture this? It was a year before the Evil Empire crumbled and fell, and old man Reagan was giving his farewell address to the United Nations. He concluded by speaking almost like a grandfather speaking directly to one his own offspring. He spoke of the birth of the United States, how Franklin had called for prayers at the Constitutional Convention, and how Washington's farewell address had spoken of God as the source of liberty, how the case for inalienable rights and "the notion of conscience above compulsion" can only be made in the context of a "higher law"! He spoke of "seeking in silence the will of Him who made us," and he spoke of Family as "the first and most important unit of society":

> "This morning, my thoughts go to her who gave me many things in life, but her most important gift was the knowledge of happiness and solace to be gained in prayer... I think then of her and others like her in that small town in Illinois, gentle people who possessed something that those who hold positions

of power sometimes forget to prize. No one of them could ever have imagined the boy from the banks of the Rock River would come to this moment and have this opportunity.

"But had they been told it would happen, I think they would have been a bit disappointed if I'd not spoken here for what they knew so well: That when we grow weary of the world and its troubles, when our faith in humanity falters, it is then that we must seek comfort and refreshment of spirit in a deeper source of wisdom, one greater than ourselves." [emphasis by me]

My own family lived for over 110 years in the Valley of the Rock and its tributaries. My grandfather once farmed right on the Rock, south of Rockford, not too many miles upstream from Dixon. My grandfather died before I was born, but he would have been so grateful that a President of the United States took time to honor the old neighborhood in the UN General Assembly Hall in New York City!

May God have mercy on Hollywood, and anyone who would slander the Reagans - or their neighbors. In "Blazing Saddles," for instance, Gene Wilder said this:

"These are the Common Clay of the Old West, farmers. You know - MORONS!"

At times such as these, when Hollywood families are the epitome of dysfunctional, it takes a lot of chutzpah for the far-out Left Coast to lecture us about "dysfunctional families"! A few years ago there was an article entitled "Hollywood Tragedies - the Price of Fame," and it mentioned such names as:

John Belushi (1949-1982), Chris Farley (1964-1997), Kurt Cobain (1967-1994), Andy Gibb (1958-1988), Mama Cass (died at 33), Freddie Prinze (1954-1977), James Dean (1931-1955), and Jayne Mansfield (1933-1967), all of whom died prematurely, most of whom contributed to their own deaths.

The story included many who succumbed to AIDS, such as, Rock Hudson (1925-1985), Liberace (1919-1987), Anthony Perkins (1932-1992), Rudolph Nureyev (1938-1993), and Arthur Ashe (1943-1993).

Famous people who lost children included Paul Newman, Carroll O'Connor, Mary Tyler Moore, Sally Jessy Raphael, Tony Curtis, Dean Martin, and others including both Johnny Carson and Ed McMahon.

Famous people who died violently: Marvin Gaye, John Lennon, Princess Grace, Selena, Montgomery Clift, Buddy Holly, Ricky Nelson, and John Denver. More than one Hollywood female has died under strange and/or violent circumstances, such as, Natalie Wood and Sharon Tate, Mrs. Robert Blake, Mrs. O.J. Simpson, and of course Marilyn Monroe.

Just plain "strange" families include the Kirk Douglas family, the Barrymores, the Fondas, and the Jackson family. Don't laugh, but this was a National Enquirer special (one of their best), and more recent tragedies since its publication would include the deaths Anna Nicole Smith and Heath Ledger.

I have had it up to my "vestigial gills" with being lectured by the Left Coast about "dysfunctional families." I have also had it up to here with politicians who claim that the Era of Reagan is over (and with the news media who claim that "family values are no longer relevant"). If Reaganism were dead, you wouldn't need a crystal ball to see where this generation would "eventuate":

In 1919, it is said, a document was discovered in Europe listing nine Communist goals, including:

> Corrupt the young: get them away from religion. Get them interested in sex. Make them superficial; destroy their ruggedness.

> Get control of all means of publicity. Get peoples' minds off their government by focusing their attention on… sexy books, plays and other trivialities ["celebrity culture"].

Divide people into hostile groups by constantly harping on controversial matters of no importance [think nicknames for sports teams].

Always preach true democracy; but seize power as fast and as ruthlessly as possible.

By encouraging government extravagance, destroy its credit; produce fear of inflation, rising prices and general discontent.

By special argument cause a breakdown of the old moral virtues; honesty, sobriety, continence, faith in the pledged word, ruggedness.

Cause the registration of all firearms on some pretext with a view of confiscation of them.

Exactly whom these goals were authored by is not certain, but they all clearly agree with the goals of the Nihilists of the "sixties" (1860s Russia) that I have already detailed.

Make no mistake about it: McCarthy alleged, and KGB documents seized after the fall of the Soviet Union substantiate, that money from the Communist Party USSR was given directly to the promotion of these goals in the U.S. - starting well before the "Youth Revolution" of the 1960s. Why do you suppose Hollywood in the early 1950s preferred "rather to be in bed with the Reds than dead"?

It is no accident that the Feminist movement followed obediently 10 paces behind the Nihilism of the 1960s, nor that the blurring of the sexes was (and still is) promoted in the name of "social equality." One can only surmise the amount of money still being dedicated to the abolition of such things as religion and "ruggedness" (Hollywood doesn't seem to mind losing money on trashy movies. Why?).

Hipper-than-thou "moderns" make fun of Ozzie and Harriet, Leave it to Beaver, and "Father Knows Best." Do not look to the media for a movement any time soon for a return to "Happy Days." Why? Follow the money. Those kinds of families don't provide much revenue for public employees in law enforcement, corrections, for courtroom bailiffs or stenographers, for lawyers or judges, for parole officers, "school psychologists," social workers, or "grief counselors" (or TV "journalists").

The "Feminazis" do not speak for all women. Maybe it's time for our "she-bears" to rise up in a counter-revolt (before both genders are ruined by the public school war on boys)! One of the Communist goals I omitted above was: "Destroy the natural leaders." Regarding which:

According to one article, the "experts" are thinking that a warning label may need to be placed on Ritalin - due to over-use and some "Ritalin patient" fatalities. - Washington Post (2/09/06)

The U.S. is about the only nation that officially recognizes AHDH as a "disorder," and yet around 10 percent of our 10-year old boys are "on" Ritalin. Again a "dumb" question is, WHY? The best guess is that educators have slowed down education so much that the brightest five percent are the ones who are "restless," and are among those who are "squirming in their seats." Thus Nurse Ratchet prescribes the Ritalin in the name of "peace," tranquility, and the lowest common denominator, but in actuality what's happening is: America's "natural leaders" of the future are being (essentially) castrated!

P.S. "A Tale of Two Women":

That reminds me of another short history story. In John Eidsmoe's book on the Founders, the first woman mentioned was the mother of John Witherspoon. He was born in Scotland in 1723, and she taught him how to read from the Bible by the age of four. The Witherspoon family had a lineage of clergymen on both sides and Mrs. Witherspoon was a descendant of John Knox. Eidsmoe says:

"Home teaching followed by grammar school prepared John for the university in Edinburgh by age thirteen. In three years he earned his

Master of Arts degree and spent four more years in Edinburgh preparing for the ministry…

"At that time Scottish Presbyterianism was split between the Moderate Party and the Popular Party. The Popular Party stressed the need for more Bible-centered sermons, less emphasis on philosophy and extra-biblical matters in church services… [and] Witherspoon became the leader of the Popular Party. Around 1753 a satire on the Moderates appeared [attributed to him]." It sold well in seven editions and nine reprints.

Despite the "controversy," he pastored a large church in Paisley for eleven years, and in 1767 was recruited by the College of New Jersey (now Princeton) to be its president. His wife did not want to leave Scotland, but she "conceded" and so, John Witherspoon ran "Princeton" for 26 years. John's wife was one of the heroes of the story, but his mother was an even bigger hero ("you shall know them by their fruits"). Now here's the "rest of the story":

From 1768 to 1794, the College produced a harvest of 478 graduates, of whom 114 became ministers, 33 became Congressmen, 20 became U.S. Senators, 13 became state governors, 3 became Justices of the U.S. Supreme Court (including John Jay, the first Chief Justice), one became Vice-President, and one (James Madison) became President of the United States, not to mention Father of the Constitution.

One might say that these were all the fruits of one woman's work of teaching one little boy how to read by the age of four. I hope I'm not boring you to tears. Wouldn't you prefer stories such as this to "The Vagina Monologues"? The morals of the story are many, including the fact that this is "not your father's Ivy League" anymore, plus the fact that the Founding Families were indeed "True Believers."

Upon disbanding the army on June 8, 1783, George Washington spoke the following words to the governors of the States:

> "I now make it my earnest prayer that God would have you and the State over which you preside, in His holy protection; that He would incline the hearts of the citizens to cultivate a spirit of

obedience to government, to entertain a brotherly affection and love for one another, for their fellow citizens of the United States at large, and particularly for their brethren who have served in the field; and, finally, that He would be most graciously pleased to dispose us all to do justice, to love mercy, and to demean ourselves with that pacific temper of mind, which were the characteristics of the Divine Author of our blessed religion."

How long will the women of the Western world stand by and watch their own kids being stupefied by the public school systems, and their boys made into castroti? The female of the species is supposedly more deadly than the male.

[Except when they're "sitting around" watching soap operas, etc. on that stupid TV. Turn it off!]

> Section 1F:
> "Just in over the transom:
> What is critical thinking?"
> www.RenewAmerica.us/
> columns/dahlgren/060728

IT STARTED OUT QUITE INNOCENTLY. I began to 'think' at cocktail parties now and then - just to loosen up. Inevitably, though, one thought led to another, and soon I was more than just a 'social' thinker. I began to think alone - "to relax," I told myself - but even then I knew it wasn't true.

"Thinking" became an obsession for me, and I couldn't get enough of the stuff. I was thinking all the time, and it began to affect my family life. One evening I had turned off the TV and asked my wife what she thought about the meaning of life. I spent that night on the couch.

I began to think on the job. I knew we weren't paid to think, but I couldn't stop myself. I began to avoid friends at lunchtime so I could read Kafka, Orwell, and Buckley. I would return to the office dizzied and confused, asking, "What is WRONG with people?"

Curtis Dahlgren

One day the boss called me in. He said, "Listen, I like you, and it hurts me to say this, but your thinking has become a real problem here. If you don't stop thinking on the job, you'll have to find another job."

This gave me a lot to think about, so I went straight home after work, and said to my wife, "Honey, I've been thinking…"

"I know you've been thinking," she said, "and I want a divorce!"

"But Honey, I don't think it's that serious."

"It's more serious than you even imagine," she said, wiping away a tear. "Your boss called and says you could lose your job. And your minister says if you don't stop your thinking, you could lose your mind! He says you can have one think a day if you must, but that's it! Tlhinking destroys brain cells."

"That's a faulty syllogism," I said. "And surely you didn't tell the minister about my thinking!"

She burst into tears and said, "We need to talk."

"But then wouldn't we both have to think?" I said, ducking to avoid my favorite thinking mug, as it crashed in pieces against the wall. "I'm going to the library," I said, after the door had safely been slammed behind me. I headed for the library, in the mood for some Tocqueville or Gibbon. I roared into the parking lot and ran up to the big glass doors.

They didn't open. It was Martin Luther King Day, so the library was closed. I believe that a Higher Power was looking out for me that night. Leaning against the unfeeling glass, thirsty for some early American history, a poster caught my eye: "Friend, is heavy thinking ruining your life?"

You probably recognize that; it comes from the standard Thinkers Anonymous poster. Which is why I am what I am today: a recovering thinker. I never miss a T&A meeting, at which we always watch a popular TV show or a movie. Last week it was "American Idol" and tonight it's going to be 60 Minutes or "Animal House."

Then we share experiences about how we avoided thinking since the last meeting. I still have my job, and things are a lot better at home. Life just seemed… somehow easier - as soon as I stopped thinking (one day at a time).

We have guest lecturers at T&A who tell us the two tell-tale signs of a "problem thinker": if you think ALONE, or you think WITH people. For shame to think I even used to think in bars! But I "think" I'm on the road to recovery.

Today I made one of the final steps. I made a contribution to the ACLU. The 12th step involves reading three New York Times editorials without throwing up. You can see why this is a life-long battle. Once a thinkaholic, always a thinkaholic. One is never 100 percent "recovered," but I'm very encouraged because I'm now watching day-time soap operas day and night. And I can say "Two plus two equals five" three times fast, without making a mistake.

P.S. The real author of that piece is unknown and is (I THINK) "anonymous." I've written more than 200 columns and I don't need to "borrow" material, but this Internet product was simply too good not to include for Posterity (at least in this 1st edition). This isn't "plagiarism." It's a clear case of copy-and-paste (with a few improvements added). It has been posted on various sites, and my hat's off to the real author. If he wishes to complain, he can call my "Risk Management" department (I wonder which one of the disciples was in charge of Risk Management - Judas?).

PPS: When the word "politics" entered the English language several centuries ago, it meant - literally – "judiciousness" so in conclusion, in light of the new three-trillion-dollar federal budget, "politics" could be changed via "creative spelling" to "poly-ticks" - meaning literally, "many blood-sucking creatures."

I "think" we've gone from the sublime to the ridiculous. Unlike Santa Claus, a government that has the power to give you everything you "ask for" is a government that has the power, through an injudicious judiciary, to take away everything you possess, including your Life, Liberty, and the Pursuit of Happiness!

Some of you may "think" that I'm trying to sell exaggerations as "literature." I do not exaggerate about something so serious as our Heritage, or the danger to it coming from pop culture and the education Establishment. For example, believe it or not, President Reagan was so hated in some circles for defending the "old ways," that his first inaugural address has even been "edited" by the Academics.

In the section where Reagan said, "Government is not the solution to our problem. Government is the problem," many university online archives blatantly deleted that second sentence! As of 2001, even Grollier's Encyclopedia was using the "censored" version. I kid you not!

PPPS: Turn off that stupid TV and finish reading the book!

Section 1G:
"Abortion is killing us"
www.RenewAmerica.us/
columns/dahlgren/030928

[I'm giving this piece priority here because the news media and politicians have almost classified abortion/euthanasia the one verboten topic. To put that in context, it is similar to the way they had hoped slavery as an issue would "just go away," before the Whig party died in the 1850s and we headed toward Civil War. The Whigs thought that they could ignore slavery because the abolitionists "had no place else to go." The People finally figured out that there was someplace else to go, and told the Whigs where to go.]

> "We are not sure that words always save, but we know, and are sure, that silence kills."
>
> - Doctors Without Borders

ACCORDING TO A POLL published May 11, 1999 (USA Today), 21% of abortion clinic patients said they didn't get enough "privacy" in recovery rooms. "Those findings are reminders that women don't see abortion as just another medical procedure," said the chairman of the department of ob-gyn at Boston Medical Center. "No one who goes in to get their gallbladder removed worries about privacy."

In the May-June 1997 issue of Ms. magazine, Faye Wattleton said, "Who believes that abortion   is something other than killing?" So, why can't we all "just get along" and agree that abortion is not "just another medical procedure"?

In his speech to the House of Representatives on September 19, 1996 Henry Hyde of Illinois said, "I finally figured out why supporters of abortion on demand fight this infanticide ban [partial-birth abortion ban] tooth and claw, because for the first time since Roe v. Wade the focus is on the baby, not the mother, not the woman but the baby, and the harm that abortion inflicts on an unborn child....

> "Dwight Eisenhower wrote about the loss of 1.2 million lives in World War II, and he said: 'The loss of lives that might have otherwise been creatively lived scars the mind of the civilized world'."

And it sears the soul when we justify the killing (Wattleton's word) of more than that many unborn babies in the U.S. - EVERY YEAR - some of them four-fifths born! Do the math! "Run the numbers"! Get mad. Show the same passion over human life that you do over tax cuts!

While we maybe "remember 9/11," most of us try to forget that more people die (babies) from abortion every day than died on September 11, 2001. That's just an "average"; actually half of the babies who die every week die on "the 7th day": some thirteen or fourteen thousand human lives lost every Saturday!

We react with euphemisms and catchwords: "Freedom to choose." "Reproductive Rights." "Womens' health." "Planned Parenthood." In other words, "don't worry be happy" - just eat, drink and be merry - for tomorrow we ALL may die?

If we can justify this we can justify post-birth abortions (and we have); and if we can justify that we can justify "assisted suicide" (and we have); and if we can justify that we can justify involuntary euthanasia (the Netherlands formalized it, and we are working on it); and if we can justify that, as Raskolnikov said in Dostoyevsky's Crime and Punishment, "Man can get used to anything, the beast!"

The pro-abortion movement will someday smother under the weight of its own "success." After World War II, which killed 50 million, America led the "sexual revolution" and most Western nations permissivized abortion-on-demand, but West Germany's highest court said, "The historical situation in the Federal Republic with the bitter experiences of the Nazi period led to the establishment of a value system in which human life has absolute priority and according to which even apparently socially unworthy life must not be destroyed."

Unbelievable? You think this is some lie from an extremist "anti-abortion rag"? NAY. This is from the pages of The Milwaukee Sentinel (March 5, 1975): "Germans Remember 1930s, Reject Abortion" by Nick Thimmesch. He said, "The extermination of 10 to 12 million people did not happen through an overnight decision by Adolf Hitler.... No, it was a group of Austrian and German physicians and jurists who came to believe, in the 1920s, that there were human lives devoid of value, and that it would be merciful to terminate those lives....

> "In May of 1935, the Hamburg Eugenics Court declared that the interruption of pregnancy for eugenic reasons (or, 'racial emergency') was exempt from punishment, thereby legalizing eugenic abortion.... There followed the 'mercy killings' of some 275,000 German 'undesirables' in state hospitals: mental patients, epileptics, encephalitics, amputees (including World War I veterans), deformed and retarded children. It was all clean, clinical and modern."

The pro-abortionists' claim that Hitler was anti-abortion is a canard; fact is, he didn't want his Aryan "Master Race" to abort, or course (the pram was the first personnel carrier of the Third Reich), but minorities were a different story! Observers of German society in the 1920s and 1930s maintain the German people did not foresee the horrible death camps but were aware of the eugenics movement and "the new attitude toward the value of human life."

A "little book" was published in 1984 entitled "Abortion and the Conscience of a Nation," by President Reagan. In the introduction to this little book, an essay by Malcolm Muggeridge says:

> "One of the great contributions of television to preparing the way for the collectivist-authoritarian way of life towards which all western countries are, in their different ways, sleep-walking, is its capacity to present consensus in terms of ostensible controversy" [i.e., Traditionalism becomes the "controversial" while change passes for "progress"].

Movies and television have told us much about the effects of the Holocaust while almost totally ignoring its origins. Muggeridge says that "In this televised version, an essential consideration has been left out - namely, that the origins of the holocaust lay, not in Nazi terrorism and anti-semitism, but in pre-Nazi Weimar Germany's acceptance of euthanasia and mercy-killing as humane...

> "Surely some future Gibbon surveying our times will note sardonically that it took no more than three decades to transform a war crime [1945] into an act of compassion [73], thereby enabling the victors in the war against Nazi-ism to adopt the very practices for which the Nazis have been solemnly condemned at Nuremberg...
>
> "It all began in the early twenties... All the most horrible and disgusting aspects of the last decades of the 20th century - the pornography, the sadism, the violence, the moral and spiritual vacuum - were already in evidence there. In this sick environment, the notion of mercy-killing was put forward in 1920 in a book

entitled The Release of the Destruction of Life Devoid of Value by Alfred Hoche, a reputable psychiatrist, and Karl Binding, a jurist...

"From these beginnings, a program of mercy-killing developed which was initiated, directed and supported by doctors and psychiatrists, some of them of considerable eminence - all this when the Nazi movement was still at an embryonic stage, and Hitler had barely been heard of...

"Subsequently, of course, the numbers of the killed rose to astronomical figures, and the medical basis for their slaughter grew ever flimsier; but it should never be forgotten that it was the euthanasia program first organized under the Weimar Republic by the medical profession, which led to and merged into the genocide program of 1941-45."

German high school math classes even "got with the program" by posing such questions as: "How many home loans for newlyweds could be paid for with the money wasted on useless eaters in our government institutions?" As history repeats, Americans turn up the "bass" on their speakers so as not to hear the silent screams, and we lose ourselves in "Entertainment du jour," as if we were kings who deserve entertaining by a joker at the snap of a finger or the click of a clacker.

By the way, Poland outlawed abortion-on-demand since Communism fell there, and women are NOT DYING FROM "COAT HANGER ABORTIONS." Germany, on the other hand, liberalized abortions after the fall of Communism.

You say you're still "pro-choice"? That's easy for you to say when you aren't the one being drawn, quartered, or sucked up a vacuum tube!

As Congressman Hyde said in 1996, "That we are even debating this issue, that we have to argue about the legality of an abortionist plunging a pair of scissors into the back of the tiny neck of a little child whose trunk, arms and legs have already been delivered, and then suctioning out his brains only confirms Dostoyevsky's harsh truth."

Man is a beast and we can get used to anything. We can even JUSTIFY it! We can even call that "LIBERTY"! America, how low can you go?

As Mordecai once told Esther, "If you hold your peace, don't think that you will escape in the king's house" any more than the rest of us. That's good advice even for those who work in the White House. The popularity of involuntary euthanasia is rising in the judiciary (Florida, for instance; the Terri Schindler case was a bad omen for all the elderly people living down there), so if you speak up, the life you save may one day be your OWN.

P.S. One of the juvenile canards of the abortion proponents is that one cannot be pro-life and favor capital punishment, but a murderer first has to be pronounced "guilty." Who's going to throw the first stone at the unborn baby? What is SHE guilty of? She didn't ask to be conceived you know. More females are aborted than boy babies, which is an ironic twist on the history of the Pharaoh of Egypt ("Every son that is born you shall cast into the river"), and on King Herod's strategy in Israel at the end of history's first Epoch (when Christ was born).

And another thing: A good rule of thumb is, if your position in an "argument" is strong enough, you have no need of misrepresenting the position of your opponents. Politicians and the media, however, insist in saying that defenders of the sanctity of human life want to "put women in jail." Preposterous! I'm old enough to remember the pre-Roe v. Wade era; and only the doctor could ever prosecuted for abortions (which were illegal - believe it or not - and "rare"). The only thing we were fighting for was the existing Law that went all the way back to time immemorial.

It's too ironical to end this section with that last word - so let me add: "Turn off that stupid TV!"

Chapter 2
Town vs. Gown: Traditional education vs. Politically correct "Higher" education -

("Trickle-down insanity")

Introduction: "The Sadducees"

"I don't need to do a better job. I just need better PR on the job I'm doing!"

— Calvin

One of the clearest indicators of the quality of our public schools is the amount of money the teachers' unions have to spend on advertising, telling us that we have "great schools." They wouldn't have to do that if people didn't know otherwise. In the old comic strip "Calvin and Hobbes," one day Hobbes was scolding Calvin and telling him he ought to do a better job cleaning up his room, and Calvin said he just needed better PR. I miss Calvin!

[I just saw a children's book on "global warming" and one of its points is, you can help stop global warming if you clean up your room!]

The education Establishment ought to save its advertising money and buy Hooked on Phonics tapes, if they were serious about improving literacy (I honestly don't believe that they are serious). You don't have to tell me, there are "many fine and competent teachers" at the K-12 level, but in many ways their hands are tied. Like the two-story outhouse, the worst stuff trickles down from the top.

I don't think the schools of education or the teachers' unions even realize, or care, but literacy and literature were extremely important to the nation until the arrival of the boob tube and "new and improved" methods of teaching reading. They even want to snuff out home-schooling. In the 1830s, Alexis de Tocqueville wrote:

> "There is hardly a pioneer's hut which does not contain a few odd volumes of Shakespeare. I remember reading the feudal drama of Henry V for the first time in a log cabin."

Having been born too soon to be put on Ritalin, I had the "mixed blessing" of being admitted to the University of Wisconsin twice, once on an ag scholarship and once as a recreation major. In 1960-61, even in the College of Agriculture, professors were making rumblings about "value judgments" (we weren't to make them), but most professors were still quite sound in their thinking. An economics professor even pointed out that Fascism (nazism) is on the Left side of the political spectrum, not on the "right." He drew it out on the blackboard like this, left to right:

> "Communism, national socialism, socialism, cooperativism, capitalism, individualism"!

In case a reader doesn't know, "Nazi" was a contraction of "National socialism," which is as close to far-left Communism as you can get. That means that when today's academics call a Traditionalist a fascist, they are flat-out lying through their teeth (see the book "Liberal Fascism" by Jonah Goldberg).

For too long, we have been "rope-a-doped." People have been looking out for Big Brother on the "right hand" for so long that we don't see the left hook coming. Too many of us don't see Political Correctness and anti-"hate speech" laws for what they are, Fascism! People are so weary of "politics" that we're on the ropes.

When I returned to Madison in 1970-71, I steeled myself to expect to hear my religious beliefs attacked before the first week was out. I was only taking a few courses, but one professor wasted no time at all, "informing" us that most of the pollution in the world was the Bible's fault (for saying "Replenish the earth and subdue it").

The only thing that shocked me was that this was in Landscaping 101, and the professor was also lauding the Eastern religions as more "friendly" (to the earth). Evidently, the Bible cannot be quoted in the classroom except to attack the Bible! The professor's point was that "subdue" (he thought) is used as an excuse to pollute, which ignores Christian stewardship, and merely means that translating words from one language to another is often a tricky proposition [it should read "manage" the earth].

I complained to the professor just for the record, but it probably didn't do much good. Let me rephrase that: Whether it does any good or not, students who know better are accountable for what they know, and a response to such professors is a requirement of the Faith.

Later in the semester, the Teaching Assistant passed around a petition for the legalization of abortion. I signed it, "R.U. KIDDINGME." I also did a little bit of writing in the Badger Herald, the new conservative alternative to the liberal student newspaper which used to have a monopoly.

Although I had once been encouraged by an economics professor to finish school, I wanted to work outdoors, so I voluntarily escaped the "Berkeley of the East" and resumed my career in tree work (we were once called tree surgeons, then "urban phytonarians"; now, "arborists").

"He who loves the beauty of trees, which God put upon this earth for us to enjoy, receives more substantial and enduring happiness for himself. He radiates something fine to the world about him and leaves mankind a little richer for his having lived."

- Martin L. Davey
(1931; the Davey Tree Radio Hour)

My career choice was a good one for my physical and spiritual health, and the work taught me many valuable lessons unavailable in the classroom. For example, when I look at a tree that needs pruning, the first question is, "What is wrong with this picture?" It was a great mental exercise, and the Davey motto was, Do it right or not at all.

"What is wrong with this picture" is the question I apply to every aspect of society, including the post-modern colleges and universities. They're "not quite right" to say the least, and need some cutting back!

P.S. I love trees - some of my best friends are trees - but liberal educators, you're no friends of trees. In the early 70s, I joined Friends of the Earth, a big ecology organization of the day. As I read my first copy of their publication, however, I didn't like the "tone" and wrote to complain about its unabashed socialist leanings. In fact, I canceled my subscription. The editor wrote a letter back and said I probably wouldn't have enjoyed the magazine much anyway, "because most ecologists are socialists"!!!

That being the case, another dumb question comes to mind: Are they ecologists because they are first socialists, or were they socialists because they are ecologists first? I suspect the former, which calls into question the genuineness of their "friendliness" to either Nature or humans. They still advocate policies in 2008 that could destroy the whole world's economy. Is that what they want? Yes - if they're socialists - and I still have that letter admitting that they ARE.

By the way, the worst examples of pollution haven't occurred in nations dominated by "Bible- thumpers," but in atheistic nations such as the old USSR and China. The Soviets even sank "hot" nuclear submarines that were out of control, not to mention Chernobyl (which is Russian for "wormwood," by the way).

P.S.: "What do you want on your Tombstone?"

> Section 2A:
> "Freshman orientation week;
> Town vs. Gown 101"
> www.RenewAmerica.us/
> columns/dahlgren/070809

"Evolution introduced a mode of thinking that in the end was bound to transform the logic of knowledge, and hence the treatment of morals, politics, and religion."

- John Dewey

OUR STUDENTS NEED HELP, but the engineers and other hard science grads have spent the last 40 years doing their own jobs, returning to campus only to stand on the sidelines cheering the football team. Too many of them don't even notice that the old alma mater has grown steadily more anti-tradition, anti-business, anti-American, and now even anti-Semitic.

According to UP magazine, Ben Stein says, "I don't like being pushed around for being a Jew, and I don't think Christians like being pushed around for being Christians. I think people who believe in God are sick and tired of getting pushed around."

At least we could HOPE so! We are about two generations too late responding to the "pushing around," but I'm re-posting the following excerpt from my favorite column, written in December 2005. I simply can't top the words in the quotations that follow:

"No man who worships education has got the best out of education... Without a gentle contempt for education no man's education is complete."

- G.K. Chesterton

"I think everyone should go to college and get a degree and then spend six months as a bartender and six months as a cab driver. Then they would really be educated."

- Al McGuire
(coach, Marquette WARRIORS)

"It is a thousand times better to have common sense without education than to have education without common sense."

- Robert Green Ingersoll

"An educated person is one who has learned that information almost always turns out to be at best incomplete and very often false, misleading, fictitious, mendacious - just dead wrong."

- Russell Baker

"It's not that our liberal friends are ignorant; it's just that they know so much that isn't so."

- Ronald Reagan

"For us in Russia communism is a dead dog. For many people in the West, it is still a log lion... Blow the dust off the clock. Your watches are behind the times. Throw open the heavy curtains which are so dear to you - you do not even suspect that the day has already dawned."

- Alexander Solzhenitsyn

"An era can be said to end when its basic illusions are exhausted."

- Arthur Miller

"Learning, n. The kind of ignorance distinguishing the studious… That which discloses the wise and disguises from the foolish their lack of understanding."

- Ambrose Bierce

"There is nothing so stupid as the educated man if you get him off the thing he was educated in."

- Will Rogers

"Soap and education are not as deadly as a massacre, but they are more deadly in the long run."

- Mark Twain

"An education isn't how much you have committed to memory, or even how much you know. It's being able to differentiate between what you know and what you don't."

- Anatole France

"Education is a progressive discovery of our own ignorance."

- Will Durant

"Education is learning what you didn't even know you didn't know… Knowledge is not simply another commodity. On the contrary, learning is never used up. It increases by diffusion and grows by dispersion."

- Daniel Boorstin

"The object of education is to prepare the young to educate themselves throughout their lives."

- Robert M. Hutchins

"Much education today is monumentally ineffective. All too often we are giving young people cut flowers when we should be teaching them to grow their own plants.

- John W. Gardner

"Education is simply the soul of a society as it passes from one generation to another."

- G.K. Chesterton

"For a country to have a great writer is like having another government. That's why no regime has ever loved great writers, only minor ones."

- Alexandr Solzhenitzyn

An inferior educational system is probably preferred today! It produces lots of "worker bees" who are the most easily manipulated for political purposes. This may sound overly-cynical, but we have stupidly left our children's souls in the hands of "professional educators" who have no intention of passing on our society's "soul" to the next generation. Lady Thatcher said:

"Be warned. A powerful, radical left-wing clerisy is bent on destroying what every past generation would have understood to be the central purpose of education - that is - allowing… individuals to 'avail themselves of the general bank and capital of nations, and of ages'… "

Generation XYZ can't make heads or tails out of Maggie's first sentence there, so they just crank up the amps on their car radios. The "soul of our society" that Chesterton was talking about is all but forgotten, and our society's "culture" - that we used to simply call Americanism - has been replaced in the public schools with social engineering toward a New World Order (as in "The world is my country")!

Conclusion:
It's alimentary, my dear Watson

Back to the present: The elitists are now saying openly that "borders are relics of a bygone era" [unless it's the Palestinian border]. The elitists are openly accusing all religious people of "anti-intellectualism" [unless you're talking about "the religion of peace" - Islam]. They claim that "diversity is wonderful" [unless you're talking about our Judeo-Christian beliefs]!

> "The last thing leftist professors want is a roomful of students who are able to argue persuasively and challenge the bias of the typical lecture hall," says Jim Nelson Black (author of "Freefall of the American University"). Black says that most American students wouldn't be able to get into college anywhere else in the world due to their lack of academic abilities.
>
> "Alas, the academy today is obsessed with the trivial and the trashy, relentlessly focused on sexual politics, and gripped by a deep antagonism to tradition that has degenerated into a new absolutism."
>
> [Black, quoted in Whistleblower magazine, 9/05]

If you still haven't been moved to action to send or print this column for young college students, perhaps you just don't realize what they're facing! Well, Black lists the following examples of the "new" absolutist-sexual agenda:

- Soap operas; U. of Wisconsin
- Queer Theory; Queer Texts, Dartmouth
- Gay Fiction; Cornell

- Unnatural Acts: Introduction to Lesbian and Gay Literature; Brown
- How to be Gay: Male Homosexuality & Initiation; U. of Michigan
- Feminist Critique of Christianity; U. of Pennsylvania

"On the first day of class, after explaining what the course would be like, [the prof] admonished us to be open to changing our views. He said, 'Check your egos at the door, because we're right and you're wrong.'"

- Abby Nye
("Fish Out of Water: Surviving and Thriving as a Christian on a Secular Campus")

Alexis de Tocqueville warned us: "Because Roman civilization perished through barbarian invasions, we are perhaps too much inclined to think that that is the only way a civilization can die."

Tony Blair said, "We will not win this battle against this global extremism unless we win it on the level of values as well as force."

At about the same time, British academia came up with a new program euphemistically called "secure values," which eliminates any teaching of right and wrong, to "relieve" schools of the need to teach British Heritage (quoted by Rush Limbaugh, 8/01/06).

Never mind Burke - even Churchill is "out" again in Britain, which is no big surprise, since he said, "Upon this battle [with Nazism] depends the survival of Christian civilization." That is considered totally gonzo in modern Academia.

Washington, Jefferson, and Adams have been "out" for a long time, of course. What a "relief" that must be to the secular materialist humanist "progressives" on our tax-payer supported campi. But enough! Enough words have been published about the contemporary scene. What we need now is some action to hold back the Hordes of the "East." Dag Hammarskjold said that "in our era, the road to holiness necessarily leads through action." It's up to you.

"What do you want on your Tombstone?"

Section 2B:
"Town vs. gown, part II"
www.RenewAmerica.us/
columns/dahlgren/070727

"When he started talking about innate differences in aptitude between men and women, I just couldn't breathe."

- Nancy Hopkins, MIT

HARVARD UNIVERSITY HAS A MODERN VERSION OF THE INQUISITION: a jihad against anyone who refuses to sing PC doxologies such as "there are no differences between the sexes." Given ex-president Larry Summers' apologies and surrender, a sheepskin from Harvard is no longer worth the paper it's written on. Much of its "learning" is now worth no more than a pocket watch that's right twice a day. In Academialand, the Truth is "relative" and "irrelevant" - but sometimes a firing offense - if it doesn't fit the fad of the moment (even if it's the president of a university who says it). Whatever became of "academic freedom," eh?

"Etymologically, a heresy is a 'choice' one makes... Greek hairesis 'choice' [is] a derivative of hairein 'take or choose.' This was applied metaphorically to a 'course of action or thought which one chooses to take,' hence a school of thought,' and, ultimately, to a 'faction' or 'sect.'...

"Another derivative of hairein, incidentally, was diairein [meaning] 'divide'..."

- John Ayto, Dictionary of Word Origins

THE LATEST CATCHWORD our students are hearing is "multicontextualism." I guess that relates to "multiculturalism," but that one lost its PR appeal. The academicians keep on teaching "tolerance for diversity" while at the same time refusing to give our young people the most important "context": the context of history. Therefore, our kids have as much "context" for current events as someone who walks into a theater near the end of a movie.

In the history of the "university," there have almost always been "two schools of thought" - except under totalitarian governments or monolithic faculties! The word division does not necessarily equate with evil; it normally equates with "academic freedom" in fact.

For example, I have never accepted the conventional wisdom that all scholars thought the world was flat before the so-called "Enlightenment." With all the mathematical skills of the ancient Egyptians, I refuse to believe that they looked at the movements of the shadow of the round earth on the moon during an eclipse and didn't have any clue as to the shape of the earth. Are you kidding me? Conventional wisdom has never even proven that "there have never been two snow flakes alike." Speaking of flakes:

My theory is that the idea that if you sailed west you'd "fall off the edge of the earth" was a PR spin by those people who already knew where all the gold was! It was "division" or "dissent" during the Middle Ages that settled many such questions - not the kind of totalitarian scholarship on display at Harvard! The "social scientists" seem to be "bothered" by the certitude and lack of grey areas in the hard sciences and math departments, so they evidently compensate and demand absolute shades of grey in the soft sciences, while insisting upon unconditional surrender to conformity.

The point is, "division" means that there is academic freedom, which produces true choice, which produces challenges, which produces more choices and, hence, true "progress" for the human race. To cut off academic choices, as the Ivy League has done, equates with regression, not "progressivism"! To try to "understand" these eggheads and get inside their pinheads could give you a headache.

"Massey-Harris 101"

"Our status quo, right or wrong?":

While we're at it, let us note here that the word "reactionary" is not a curse word, nor does "conservative" always mean defense of the status quo! In the 1960s, the Civil Rights movement was anti-status quo, but the conservatives' concerns had more to do with HOW TO DO IT (without the curse of "excess rising expectations" burning down Watts, Newark, Detroit, and so on, which resulted).

In the 21st century, the roles have been reversed regarding the "status quo": The liberals defend the status quo of the 1960s-style nanny state, while the conservatives are proposing the anti-status quo ideas - such as school choice - and by opposing the discredited fads of progressive methodologies (think phonics versus ebonics). "Every child should have the chance to go to college," the liberals say, but given the quality of that "education," a lot of college grads are out there asking, "Do you want fries with that?" OR, "What do you want on your Tombstone?"

> Section 2C:
> "When political science fiction
> meets the freshman class"
> www.RenewAmerica.us/
> columns/dahlgren/060107

"Tears are often the telescopes through which men see far into heaven."

- Henry Ward Beecher (1813-1887)

GOLDA MEIR WOULD HAVE BEEN CLEANING HOUSE ABOUT NOW. No - I mean that in the most literal sense. When there was a big decision to be made, Golda, it is said, would go home and do house cleaning until the Right Thing would come to mind. She wouldn't consult a focus-group study, take a poll, or send up a trial balloon.

The "science" of political science has become too cute by far, and Higher Education has gotten too "high" for its own good. On the one hand, talk about "diversity" is all the rage, but on the other hand, conformity is the name of the game! It stomps out all diversity, and simple proven principles are laughed out of school.

> "Whoso would be a man must be a nonconformist… What I must do is all that concerns me, not what people think."
>
> - Ralph Waldo Emerson (1803-1882)

Years ago, a professor in Chicago on the first day of class would tell his students that they could not consider themselves to be really 'educated' unless they could answer "Yes" to the following questions:

> -"Can you look an honest man or a pure woman straight in the eye?"
> -"Will a lonely dog follow you down the street?"
> -"Do you think washing dishes or hoeing corn is as compatible with high thinking as piano playing or golf?"
> -"Could you be happy alone?"
> -"Can you look into the sky at night and see beyond the stars?"
>
> [excerpted from "Leaves of Gold," 11th edition (subtitled "An Anthology of Prayers, Memorable Phrases, Inspirational Verse and Prose from the Best Authors of the World, Both Ancient and Modern")]

Maybe if we had more good "Prose" in our lives, we wouldn't need so much Prozac (or clinics to teach us "how to sleep"). Many a tear has been shed since we stopped looking "beyond the stars" into heaven. If tears were telescopes, September 11, 2001 should have brought God into very sharp focus, but instead, our "popular culture" and the media have moved us totally in the opposite direction. I'm talking about music, the movies and TV, video games, and almost any form of entertainment you could mention. Even athletes are becoming more fierce and vicious, politics is now war, and the "news" has become a propaganda game.

Higher education considers itself the very avant-garde or vanguard of "societal evolution," but radio host Michael Savage says that society has "sunk to a point lower than Rome or the Weimar Republic in Germany." I agree, and so would the writers in "Leaves of Gold":

> "Educate men without religion and you make them but clever devils."
> - Duke of Wellington

> "True religion is the foundation of society. When that is once shaken by contempt the whole fabric cannot be stable or lasting."
> - Edmund Burke (1729-1797)

> "Learning is not wisdom: knowledge is not necessarily vital energy. The student who has to cram through a school or college course, who has made himself merely a receptacle for the teacher's thoughts and ideas, is not educated; he has not gained much. He is a reservoir, not a fountain. One retains, the other gives forth."
> - J.E. Dinger

An anonymous author in "Leaves of Gold" gets down to the "nitty-gritty":

> "Few things could be culturally more deplorable than that today the average college graduate, who fancies himself educated, should never have read the book of Job, should be unfamiliar with Isaiah, and should be hardly able to identify those mighty men of valor, Joshua, Gideon, [etc.]… For this is nothing less than a loss of racial memory, a forgetfulness of our cultural heritage that is as serious in the life of nations as is for the individual the loss of personality attendant upon neurotic disease."

Some of these professors wouldn't even be able to look a lonely dog in the eye.

Curtis Dahlgren

Like the two-story outhouse, trickle-down education starts with "higher" education, and the education departments "teach the teachers" on a need-to-know basis. If kids don't "feel like" learning a long list of spelling words, then they don't "need to know" that; just teach a shorter list of "essential" spelling words. If kids don't feel like learning fractions and multiplication tables, then just let them use a calculator. If "rote memorization" is deemed the lowest form of learning, then that's as good an excuse as any for not teaching history anymore.

The politically "correct" subjects are mandated, but "heaven forbid" that any student should be offended by the history of Western Civilization. Even the seminaries are being run into the ground.

> "A hallmark of modern liberal theology is that the search for truth is more important than the truth itself. 'Searching for truth' is an existential delight, and for a liberal, it saves you from having to take a firm position on anything."
>
> - Steven F. Hayward

What do you want on your Tombstone?

Section 2D:
"Over the transom again: Holiday letter from the Alumni Association"
www.RenewAmerica.us/
columns/dahlgren/071218

"Press 1 for English." - your friendly local undertaker's answering machine

'TIS THE SEASON FOR GIFT-GIVING. I recently received a letter from one of my alma maters begging for a gift. The words that follow are the "exact words" of their introductory remarks:

"Please accept with no obligation, explicit or implicit, our best wishes for an environmentally conscious, socially responsible, mellow but non-addictive, gender-neutral celebration of the winter solstice, practiced within the most appropriate preferences of your religious persuasion, and/or secular practices of your choice, with respect for the religious/secular persuasion and/or practices of others, or their choice not to practice religious or secular traditions at all. [Merry Christmas]

"We also wish you a fiscally successful, personally fulfilling, and medically uncomplicated recognition of the generally accepted calendar year 2008, but not without due respect for the calendars of choice of other cultures whose contributions to society have helped make America great (not to imply that America is necessarily any greater than other countries, nor the only America in the Western Hemisphere - nor to imply that unequal financial gain is necessarily a good thing) without regard to the race, creed, color, age, physical ability, religious faith, political persuasion, or sexual preference(s) of the wishee - excepting of course, if you are a woman, a minority member, or any other victim of American imperialism; in that case, you should multiply this wish by a factor of 1.759331. AND DON'T START WITH US!

"By accepting these greetings you are accepting these terms: This greeting is subject to clarification or withdrawal. It is freely transferable with no alteration to the 'original intent.' It implies no promise by the wisher to actually implement any of the wishes for himself or others, and is void where prohibited by law and is revocable at the sole discretion of the wisher. This wish is warranted to perform as expected within the usual application of good tidings for a period of no more than one year, while supplies last, or until the issuance of a subsequent greeting, whichever comes first, and warranty is limited to replacement of this wish or issuance of a new wish at the sole discretion of the wisher. Wishees are likewise advised to exercise mature reader discretion.

"This wish may be copied only in its entirely, with explicit attribution. Any personal misuse of the descriptions and accounts of this greeting are, well - DON'T EVEN THINK ABOUT IT, OKAY?" [Happy New Year]

Evidently, this fund-raising letter had been checked out by their "Risk Management" department and/or the ACLU, and needless to say, I didn't send them a check.

P.S. Seriously, neither of my alma maters actually sent this "greeting." This is just a shameless reposting of my "First annual solstice letter" from last year, and I "sort of stole" some of those words from an anonymous Internet thing that has been going around for some time (with a few personal embellishments, of course). I would have cleared this proposed opinion piece with my personal "Risk Management team," but they refuse to take my calls.

[What do you want on your Tombstone?]

Section 2E:
"The social engineers: Brilliant people or just 'primordial pond scum'?"
www.RenewAmerica.us/
columns/dahlgren/071114

"You wondered whether... the worst enemies of civilization might not prove to be its petted intellectuals who attack it at its weakest moments - attacked it in the name of reason and in the name of irrationality... in the name of sex, in the name of perfect and instant freedom."

- Saul Bellow, "Mr. Sammler's Planet" (quoted by Chas. Sykes)

PARADOXICALLY (and predictably), the "perfect and instant sexual freedom" promoted by our 65-year-old hippie pinheads has led to more and more government, and less and less real individual freedom. By its fruits, the Great Society can now be officially declared a FLOP. It used to be a maxim: "Question authority." But now that the hippies are running the asylums, they say that we can "Stop questioning authority!" So the Establishment educators and media try to distract us with talk about greenhouse gases and "man-made global warming."

[As I'm proofreading this, on the 11th of March, 2008, the temperature outside is almost zero and the snow is knee deep. I'm afraid that the farmers aren't going to get their oats in the ground in March this year like they used to do in the good old days. Even Al Gore's tobacco fields are under a blanket of snow this week, and Columbus, Ohio got 20 inches of snow.]

In an election year, we ought to have been talking about the fact that we have more murders in a year in the United States than during all the years of the "Wild, Wild West." These are the fruits of Woodstock and Berkeley and our popular culture - because there are laws of cause and effect, including "the Law of Unintended Consequences." Politicians promise "solutions" for every problem from poverty to the warming of the polar caps on Mars, but maybe they should start with a smaller problem: THEMSELVES. The decline and fall of nations don't happen over night, you know.

A Little Review Of Our History: "Power Corrupts":

Absolutely!

As a consequence of Political Correctness, an independent photographer in New Mexico was recently arrested for NOT agreeing to photograph a lesbian civil union ceremony. This is "civil liberty"? You can't say we weren't warned. In his Farewell Address (which liberals selectively refer to on rare occasions), George Washington said:

> "The spirit of encroachment tends to consolidate the powers of all the departments in one, and thus to create whatever the form of government, a real despotism. A just estimate of that love of power, and proneness to abuse it, which predominates in the human heart is sufficient to satisfy us of the truth of this position."

Before the American Revolution, the way had been prepared by a "great spiritual awakening."

In the 1830s and forties, America witnessed a sort of Second Great Awakening. The churches brought the festering sore of slavery to the attention of the general population. The elite political class, of course, desperately tried to side-step the issue by occasionally throwing a bone to the abolitionists while banning anti-slavery materials from the U.S. mails (the Gag Rules of 1835-44, with the approval of the Whig party). The members of the party who were opposed to the spread of slavery to the Territories were called "one-issue voters" who were ruining the chances of the other wing of the party for achieving political victory. [Think abortion today, or border security.]

Pure political power, rather than Washington's warning, became their obsession. In 1852, the Whigs nominated a military hero and former prisoner-of-war, General Winfield Scott, because he was thought to be "electable." Alas, the results were not as anticipated: two Democratic Presidents, Franklin Pierce and James Buchanan, the latter being a disaster (he supported the pro-slavery "special interests" and couldn't figure out what the big deal was about the new Republican party movement). The Whigs had long since whithered on the vine (though at first unsuccessful, the Republicans ran General Fremont for President in 1856).

Is History Being Repeated?

Following the Civil War and many years of domination by the Republicans, the country's zeal began to turn to apathy again. Here are a few lines from the 1992 book by Charles J. Sykes, "A Nation of Victims":

> "As the mainline churches fell into decline [the late 1800s], there was an upsurge in spiritualism... and New Thought... By the time Freudianism first arrived here, Americans were already well-disposed to listen; the groundwork had been thoroughly laid... Social Darwinism and the rise of an insatiable consumer society - a culture of expectations and entitlements - were the flotsam and jetsam of the triumph of science over faith...

"... Filling the vacuum created by the decline of institutional faith and the collapse of the moral order it has provoked, PSYCHOANALYSIS has assumed many of the functions traditionally performed by religion... Freud himself set the tone for the assault on faith. He regarded religion in all its forms as an illusion and therefore recast it as a form of neurosis... an instance of mental disorder - of madness."

Sykes writes that this New Establishment didn't need to debate the strictures of family identity or religious faith or sexual morality when they could simply be "dismissed" as products of the 'authoritarian syndrome.' An unsophisticated... or backward-looking populace hardly needed to be argued with when it could be "cured"! [my emphasis]

"By identifying the 'liberal personality' as the antithesis of the authoritarian personality, [the Intelligentsia] equated mental health with an approved political position."

- T.W. Adorno in "The Authoritarian Personality" (1950) [quoted by Sykes]

In an 11/11/07 column by Mike Heath, "The Sexual Revolution Costs Us Much," he says:

"The unrelenting campaign to loosen sexual morals derives its name from a book written by Wilhelm Reich in 1929, which was entitled, appropriately enough, 'The Sexual Revolution.' The original title was 'Sexuality in the Culture War.'

"In the book, Wilhelm Reich - a disciple of Sigmund Freud - set forth his program for radicalizing society by undermining sexual morality. Central to the thinking of Reich was the idea that conservative political views have their origin in the repression of sexuality in the child by an authoritarian father. With time, the conservative ideology becomes incorporated in the character of the child. Character, for Reich, was a bad thing.

"To change an individual's political viewpoint from conservatism to liberalism, the character of the individual must be altered or destroyed through sexual liberation. According to Reich, the path to a better world lies through the loosening of sexual morality - in others words, a sexual revolution."

Alfred Kinsey later became the icon of this "liberation movement," while John Dewey's "progressive education" took over the public schools. [The logical extension of this old, old game is the news report that a public school board in Maine voted to offer free birth control (behind the backs of parents) to 11-year-old girls! Charlie Sykes wrote a column in which he suggested that if you know a male who is having sex with an 11-year-old girl, call 911 and her parents, not the school nurse, because "a crime is being committed." Freudian political correctness has now reached the point at which it is "appropriate" to use a fifth grader like an animal (as long as the couple doesn't light up a cigarette afterwards)!]

P.S. That reminds me; some otherwise fine Traditionalists in the "culture wars" don't want to have anything to do with the Intelligent Design/Creationist battle with those same liberals (even though Darwinism is the "rock-bed" foundation for all modern forms of liberalism).

Yea for the fact that some of our female pundits have more courage to speak out than most of our male "conservatives." On the back cover of Ann Coulter's 2006 book, "Godless," it says:

"For liberals, evolution is the touchstone that separates the enlightened from the benighted. But Coulter neatly reverses the pretense that liberals are rationalists guided by the ideals of free inquiry and the scientific method. She exposes the essential truth about Darwinian evolution that liberals refuse to confront: it is bogus science."

Theistic evolutionists and/or commentators lacking the courage to touch the subject with a ten-foot pole need to review the history of our Western Civilization. Here's the "good stuff":

"Many today assume Darwin was the originator of the idea of evolution, but the concept had actually been around as early as Greek times [and]... Charles was familiar with his grandfather's writings on evolution."

[The Good News magazine, July-Aug. 07] www.gnmagazine.org

The Darwin family was actually quite a strange one. The Good News reminded me that "ironically, some might say Darwin was a victim of his own theory of natural selection because of the genetic dangers of inbreeding.

"In 1839, he married Emma, his first cousin. Both families had intermarried through first cousins for some time... [talk about Rednecks!] Twenty-six children were born from these first-cousin marriages; 19 were sterile and five died prematurely, including Darwin's daughter and first son. Many suffered from mental retardation or other hereditary illnesses, as was the case with his last son. All these effects engendered great hostility toward the idea of a personal, intervening God." [see also, "Darwin: The Life of a Tormented Evolutionist" (1992) by Adrian Desmond and James Moore]

"He was an embittered atheist, the sort who does not so much disbelieve in God as personally dislike Him." [George Orwell wrote those words (about someone).]

As for "Grampa Erasmus" Darwin (1731-1802), the Encyclopaedia Britannica (1910) says:

"The fame of Erasmus Darwin as a poet rests upon his Botanic Garden, though he also wrote The Temple of Nature, or the Origin of Society... and The Shrine of Nature.

"The Botanic Garden... is a long poem... The artificial character of the diction renders it in emotional passages stilted and even absurd... Gnomes, sylphs and nereides are introduced on almost every page, and personification is carried to an extraordinary excess. Thus he describes the Loves of the Plants according to the Linnaean system by means of a most ingenious but misplaced and amusing personification of each plant, and often even of the parts of the plant... [if you get the picture]

"In 1799 Darwin published his Phytologia, or the Philosophy of Agriculture and Gardening, in which he states his opinion that plants have sensation and volition."

POINT IS: The Darwin family's opinion was that plants have "will" - but their Designer and Creator do not! "They worship the creation more than the Creator," as Romans 1 puts it. As old Erasmus wrote in Zoonomia (1896):

"Would it be too bold to imagine that, in the great length of time since the earth began to exist, perhaps millions of ages before the commencement of the history of mankind, -would it be too bold to imagine that all warm-blooded animals have arisen from one living filament... with the power of acquiring new parts... thus possessing the faculty of continuing to improve by its own inherent activity, and of delivering down these improvements by generation to its posterity, world without end."

Charles Darwin, the grandson, was a contemporary of Abraham Lincoln, the two having been born on the same day in 1809 (the irony gets thicker and thicker, the more you study Darwinism). Yes, just "imagine" this:

The Good News writes: "As he mused over evolution, then called transmutation, Darwin started to question the need for a Creator God. He began to write some secret notebooks on the subject, afraid to divulge his radical ideas. For a country gentleman with a Christian wife and many Christian friends, he wanted to keep his heretical thoughts to himself."

In this, Charles was not unlike some males today who feign affection for radical feminism, in the quest for the "perks" of heterosexuality. But Darwin's hunger for attention - and "relevance" - eventually won out over his reluctance. The rest is history, as they say, but he owed a lot of his fame to the quirky quality of Anglo-Saxons for loving "Celebrity Culture" (think: the "Princess Diana" phenomenon).

Charlie Darwin was the Britney Spears (B.S.) of his day, propelled to fame by the insatiable appetite of human nature for "something NEW" and "cool chic" (posing as intellectual)! Now, Thomas Jefferson was no slouch (he could read in at least four languages), but believe it or not, Mr. Ripley, old Tom was a proponent of the theory of "intelligent" Design. He had heard it all in his life, but said in a letter to John Adams:

> "I hold (without appeal to revelation) that when we take a view of the Universe, in its parts general or particular, it is impossible for the human mind not to perceive and feel a conviction of design, consummate skill, and indefinite power in every atom of its composition."

If you're not afraid of some further reading material, I recommend at this point:

1) A book: "The Edge of Evolution: The Search for the Limits of Darwinism" by Michael Behe

2) A website: <http://nobelists.net/> [quotations of Nobel Prize winning scientists who believe in God]

3) One example:

> "The first gulp from the glass of natural sciences will turn you into an atheist, but at the bottom of the glass God is waiting for you."
> - Werner Heisenberg (from Does God Exist, Sept/Oct 07) www.doesgodexist.com

4) One speech: The address by French President Sarkozy to a joint session of Congress (as reported by www.RushLimbaugh.com): "To

Curtis Dahlgren

the millions of men and women who came from every country of the world and who - with their own hands, their intelligence, and their hearts - built the greatest nation in the world, America did not say, 'Come, and everything will be given to you.' Rather, she said, 'Come, and the only limits to what you will be able to achieve will be those of your own courage, your boldness, and your talent.'"

5) One article: "Movin' On Up" by the Wall Street Journal (as reported by Rush) re "the rich get richer and the poor get poorer":

> "In John Edwards' 'two Americas,' which America had the greatest percentage change in income? Don't bet the farm on the richest. You'd be wrong. It's the poorest. The lowest quintile, the liberals' losers in the lottery of life, the lowest one-fifth of earners, their median income over the last ten years increased by 90%. Well, how about the highest fifth, the quintile with the Clintons in it and me? It went up by 10%. Percentage income, 10% increase over the last ten years in the highest quintile. Lowest quintile, 90% increase over the last ten years. Now, are you surprised about this? Some of you probably are, because if you read the Drive-By newspapers, you're shocked."

Economics education in America is virtually non-existent in the public schools, of course, but so goes social engineering. As it was "back in the gool ol' USSR," some of the worst elements of society now "rule." The cream can't rise to the top anymore because the parasitic pond scum does - especially in the soft sciences of higher education. In the Arthur Voobis book about Estonia, he recounted the early days of Totalitarianism (which is where Academia has us headed):

> "Soon after these hordes conquered our country, they began, like an hungry colossus, to swallow everything they could. Farms and factories were emptied, private and state property was robbed, economic life completely upset. Overnight all became slaves...
>
> "In the very early days we saw the Communist regime establish an immediate kinship with people of a criminal past. We saw it use for its purposes only the dark elements who, in a cultural

society, hide themselves in the back alleys of a community, men whose lives are a mass of lies, deceit, treachery, and murder.

"Those with this sinister background are useful tools in the Communist system in which bestiality becomes the principle of life and crime the norm of existence. They were put in police and administrative posts and became leaders and trustees in every field...

"Education was made into something ridiculous, a mechanism for political ideology and atheistic intoxication. The lives of little children were stage-managed to absorb the atheist spirit. Even the children instinctively perceived the perversity of this system. There was such heroism in the conduct of the Estonian children, and many of them were murdered because their unconscious, simple normality reacted against such maliciousness."

So, what do you want on their Tombstones?

Section 2F:
"A-mentia: Back to school
(brainwash and tax to the max)"
www.RenewAmerica.us/
columns/dahlgren/060324

"I can live with the robber barons, but how do you live with these pathological radicals?"

- Daniel Patrick Moynihan

IN OUR CONTINUING SOAP OPERA, "GOWN vs. TOWN," today's episode comes straight from the horse's mouth. The alumni association's "ON WISCONSIN" arrived the other day with a cover story entitled, "The Year of Unfortunate Events," by Michael Penn.

The article's subhead says, "During 2005, UW-Madison endured a string of bad news that frustrated its leaders and strained relations with state legislators. Can the university calm the stormy waters? Or are there more clouds on the horizon?"

The events of 2005 included a vice chancellor's relationship with a graduate student. When the relationship went south, he took a "medical leave" to sort things out, and kept drawing his salary for nine months on a $190,000 per year job (a job the chancellor suddenly eliminated). The vice chancellor was given a "fall-back job" at $73,000 a year, but he soon left for greener pastures.

Three other UW faculty members were convicted of felonies between March and August of 2005, one for "sexually assaulting three young girls and another for e-mailing sexually explicit material to a teenage boy." But as the article says, "Because state law prohibits the university from firing an employee solely on the basis of a criminal conviction, all three cases remained wrapped up in university investigations and appeals even months after the professors were sentenced for their crimes."

Sifting and winnowing the truth - in Madison - has become "sorting things out" in the everlasting grey-zone. Taking your tenure to jail with you says a lot about the "non-judgmentalism" typical of society in general. These days, you can kill your five children in a bathtub and be given two or three trials. A female teacher can have a "relationship" with a 14-year-old boy and have all charges dropped. You can kill your newborn, but no charges are even filed sometimes.

On the other hand, a state legislator can be sent to jail for 16 years for a technicality, and two Border Patrol agents get 11 to 12 years for trying to stop a drug smuggler? But wait, there's more: In this litigious society, environmentalists have made it a Federal offense to kill certain flies and rats, but an abortionist who flushed dead babies down the toilet got in trouble only because of possible pollution of the river! And our border becomes a sieve!

Meanwhile back on Bascom Hill, concern is expressed about "morale" among the UW employees. One thing that should "help" is the $700/month "automobile allowance" that chancellors of the UW System receive. Or the guaranteed "back-up positions" that 1,092 employees enjoy in case they "screw up" on their main job.

And What Do The Taxpayers Get From Such Highly-paid Academics?

To answer the question, a whacked-out Colorado professor was paid to speak at the UW-Whitewater campus this year, and the UW-Eau Claire administrators (sieg heil) ruled that a Resident Assistant was verboten from holding voluntary Bible study sessions in his room.

As the Foundation for Individual Rights in Education puts it, "Universities often can't defend in public the policies they adopt [and which "sounded so good at the time"] in the shadowy, ivory, halls of academia." [quoted from NewsMax.com]

There is a disconnect between Main Street and the incestuous University Avenue - and the "cognitive dissonance" isn't all between the ears of us yahoos. WE AREN'T THE ONES TRYING TO SILENCE ALL OPPOSITION.

As the NewsMax article said, "When universities are offended by what students say or do… the schools often accuse them of 'harassment' - a catchword for speech that others find offensive [such as "Bible study"]. They also sometimes accuse them of 'disruption' or 'intimidation' [as if no professor ever really intimidated a Christian!]."

Constitutionally required legislative oversight, of course, is virtually non-existent. They call that "fascism." Thus, this trickle-down insanity continues to down-trickle from the Board of Regents to the Law and education schools to the high schools, and so on, all the way down to the latest wonder-of-the-world, "four-year-old kindergarten."

Someone once said that "despotism begins in the nursery school," but in actuality it all begins in the University.

Curtis Dahlgren

No Wonder We Seniors Become Grouchy Old Men, And We "Ramble."

This is what I want on my Tombstone:

He was just a post-hole digger (a PhD)
But he wasn't born yesterday!

Section 2G:
"The History of the University 101"
www.RenewAmerica.us/
columns/dahlgren/051208

"Those who can, do; those who can't, teach; those who can't teach, teach teachers."

- unknown

[I think I've stumbled upon a new way of teaching history. Most history textbooks start from the "Big Bang" and one-celled critters, and proceed through the "cave man" days, and so on, down to the present. However, I started out with the contemporary scene and went back for context to the hippies of the 1960s. Then I went back to their progenitors in 1860s Russia. Then I went back to the contrarian geniuses of 1776, and then for context back to the English thinkers who influenced the American Revolution (all the way back to the 1400s). In this section, I will trace the history of Academia back to the Greek and Roman heydays. Learning will always be work, hard work, but this method actually makes history exciting!]

"The people applaud me because everyone understands me, and they applaud you because no one understands you."

- Charlie Chaplin, to Albert Einstein

TO HEAR THEM TELL THE STORY, the intellectuals rode into town on a white charger and saved the world from the "flat-earthers" and the Dark Ages a few hundred years ago, although Christopher Columbus, who actually put his butt on the line to prove the world was round, has been made into an anti-hero by said intellectuals. Like, "HUH?"

The history of the "university" is a fascinating subject, and to put it FRANKLY, the "increase" in knowledge in the Western world probably had more to do with the repelling of the Mongols and the Arabian hordes - and one man's idea that produced the printing press - than with any sudden flashes of "brilliance" in the intellectual class.

The Encyclopaedia Britannica (11th edition) says, "In order to understand the conditions under which the earliest universities came into existence, it is necessary to take into account, not only their organization, but also of their studies, and to recognize the main influences which, from the 6th to the 12th centuries, served to modify both the theory and practice of education… The schools of the Roman Empire (6th century), which had down to that time kept alive the traditions of pagan education, had been almost entirely swept away by the barbaric invasions.

"The latter century [12th] marks the period when the institutions that replaced them - the episcopal schools attached to the cathedrals and the monastic schools - attained to their highest degree of influence and reputation… But between the pagan system and the Christian system by which it had been superseded there existed something that was common to both: the latter could not altogether dispense with the ancient text-books, simply because there were no others in existence." [article, "Universities"] And that explains a lot about the survival of paganism in some aspects of the church.

Academia's Version Of The "Enlightenment" Is Mostly Revisionism

There have always been studium and discipulorum going all the way back to the Greek and Persian and Babylonian empires, and in the revised version of history, the Intelligentsia seldom mention the role of the churches in higher education, nor the clashes between the "university" and the common (tax paying) citizens - the "townies."

The famous universities of Europe predate the Middle Ages and even much of the so-called Dark Ages. The university at Salerno, Italy was a well-known school of medicine by the 800s AD. The Britannica says that "the most authoritative researches point to the conclusion that the medical system of Salerno was originally an outcome of the Graeco-Roman tradition of the old Roman world."

Wall Of "Separation Of University And State" Torn Down:

The introduction of the role of the State into higher education occurred at the university in Bologna, with the arrival of Frederick I from Germany as Emperor of the revived "Holy Roman Empire." The Britannica says:

> "When [Frederick] marched his forces into Italy on his memorable expedition of 1155, and reasserted those imperial claims which had so long lain dormant, the professors of the civil law and their scholars, but more especially the foreign students, gathered round the Western representative of the Roman Caesars, and besought his intervention in their favor in their relations with the citizens of Bologna... [and] he granted the foreign students substantial protection, by conferring on them certain special immunities and privileges...
>
> "In them we may discern the precedent for that state protection of the university which, however essential at one time for the security and freedom of the teacher and the taught, has been far from proving an unmixed benefit - the influence which the civil power has thus been able to exert being too often wielded for the suppression of that very liberty of thought and inquiry from which the earlier universities derived in no small measure their importance and their fame."

The University And The State Combine Forces Against The Taxpayer:

Theological lectures were instituted at Oxford, England as early as 1133 AD and within about 100 years, a king-and-academia partnership began to take advantage of the locals. Again, the Britannica says:

> "The historian, John Richard Green, epitomizes the relation between the two [city and school] when he shows that 'Oxford had already seen five centuries of borough life before a student appeared within its streets... The University found Oxford a busy, prosperous borough, and reduced it to a cluster of lodging-houses. It found it among the first of English municipalities, and it so utterly crushed its freedom that the recovery of some of the commonest rights of self-government has only been brought about by recent [1825] legislation.'" [ibid, "Oxford"]

It goes on to say, "As to the relations between the university and the city, in 1248 a charter of Henry III afforded students considerable privileges at the expense of townsfolk, in the way of personal and financial protection. Moreover, the chancellor already possessed juridical powers; even over the townsfolk he shared jurisdiction with the mayor.

> "Not unnaturally these peculiar conditions engendered rivalry between 'town and gown'; rivalry led to violence, and after many lesser encounters a climax was reached on St. Scholastica's and the following day, February 10th and 11th, 1354/55. Its immediate cause was trivial, but the townsmen gave rein to their long-standing animosity, severely handled the scholars, killing many, and paying the penalty, for Edward III gave the university a new charter enhancing its privileges."

No wonder the intellectual class considers itself so important and its arrogance so "normal": IT'S AN OLD TRADITION, and tax-payer revolts are either ignored or the tax payer has to suffer "pay back."

Curtis Dahlgren

Send In The Clowns:

Modern-day manifestations of the arrogance of the old British intelligentsia include irrevocable tenure, lots of the actual teaching load shifted to "Teaching Assistants," paid "sabbaticals" and back-up jobs for those "fired" for gross violations of ethics, and humongous salaries for administrators (many including a house and a car plus expenses); second incomes and double-dipping for retirement accounts, etc. - not to mention the political clout - including the cultural power to make life miserable for the "politically incorrect townsfolk" through hate-speech codes and laws, biased journalists, student fees to fund pet PC projects, and of course, "environmentalism," etc.! It's enough to make a grown man cry, or maybe even upset the staid, cool English - "given enough time!"

Early History Of The University In America:

The Britannica says [article, "University"], "Harvard, William and Mary, and Yale, the three pioneers of colonial times, were organized in the days of colonial poverty, on the plans of the English colleges which constitute the universities of Oxford and Cambridge. Graduates of Harvard and Yale carried these British traditions to other places, and similar colleges grew up in New York, New Jersey, Pennsylvania, New Hampshire, and Rhode Island, and later in many other states…

"The underlying principle in these institutions was discipline - mental, moral and religious" Believe it or not, Mr. Ripley! [ibid, with added emphasis and personal comment]

"Whazzup?": The Present Chaos:

Two Texas university student groups set up "Smut for smut" booths at school - at which they gave out pornographic literature for every Bible turned in (sort of like a "gun buy-out" program with a twist). San Diego university students produce and star in their own XXX rated videos over the school cable system. Certain words are verboten on campuses from sea to shining sea, especially if the first 6 letters in the word are "Christ"! Gay groups tap into the "student fee" funds, but conservative papers published with private funds are stolen and burned, or sometimes banned. Of course, Ann Coulter and Laura Ingraham, et al, do not have full "First Amendment" rights anymore on the college campi. They even get "intimidated" and "harassed" (though not silenced YET).

Is There Any "Hope"?

It may be far too little, far too late, but just a glimmer of hope appeared the other day. I heard that National Public Radio now offers some token Traditionalist pundits, and in 2006 it was announced that the Harvard Law School was diversifying its professorships, under a new multi-million-dollar program. New professors are to be hired on academic skills - regardless of ideology! This will not only reduce teacher-to-student ratios, but may allow a conservative or two to sneak in the back door.

On the flip side, it may just mean more graduates of Harvard Law (the last thing this country needs)!But it's a start. Eventually, this may bring back the old, old "two schools of thought" concept, which Political Correctness has all but obliterated. Do you suppose Academia senses a revolt by the Townies coming again? Maybe they're not as "deaf and stumm" as they seem!

College Textbook Selection:

In "This Beat Working For a Living," Professor X, a history professor, explains the "textbook phenomenon" in our colleges and universities:

> "Once the professor has gathered sample copies of possible textbooks for his course, he has the choice of selection... Certainly it is not the readability of the book that counts. In fact, I have observed that the more literary (readable) a book is, the less likely

it is to be adopted. I think that intuitively professors shy away from well-written books because they realize that their lectures suffer by comparison...

"More than anything else it will be selected on the basis of the image of the author. You see, the big names in any discipline get an image, and here I mean politically and socially. Inasmuch as most professors are liberal, they select textbooks written by men with a liberal image...

"The result is that most of them are wretchedly written, dull, ponderous - and liberal. The students' salvation resides in the fact that most do not read the things, and few of the remainder understand what they have read."

A few appropriate closing quotations:

"A bad book is as much a labor to write as a good one, it comes as sincerely from the author's soul."

- Aldous Huxley

"In Russia when you answer questions, you may come to an unfortunate conclusion."

- Aleksandr Solzhenitzyn

"A dead thing can go with the stream, but only a living thing can go against it."

- G.K. Chesterton

Enough Said On The Subject Of Education?

P.S. I wouldn't expect this book to be selected for required reading any time soon - sometimes I wonder "why bother?"- but even if we fail to save education from itself, someday people will wonder what went so horribly wrong, and how it happened. NOW YOU KNOW.

"Massey-Harris 101"

"What do <u>you</u> want on <u>your</u> Tombstone?" [Tombstone pizza, that is.]

PPS: Here's what you can put on my tombstone ("that'll be the day").

When I am dead, I hope it may be said:
'His sins were scarlet, but his books were read.'

I stole that from Hilaire Belloc (1870-1953), a man whose "dash between the years" stretched from shortly after Lincoln's assassination to the year I saw my first major league baseball game between the Milwaukee Braves and the Philadelphia Phillies. Speaking of "phillies" (I ramble), that's also about the time I saw the last game played by the Rockford Peaches. Not to go autobiographical on you, but my dad even had a cousin who was on the board of directors for the Peaches (of "A League of Their Own" movie fame).

Now as I recall, those were some appealingly skirted yet "strong" women (the catcher for the Peaches hit a home run over the right field fence). It's a paradox again. Today's feminists have turned the world upside down. They wouldn't even be able to lay sod and get the "green side up." They're even trying to fight the importation of women from northeastern Europe because they make wives who are "too feminine." That reminds me of a quote:

Mae West said, "The best way to hold a man is in your arms." But times change.

Andy Warhohl said, "I always run into strong women who are looking for weak men to dominate them." But enough of this.

By rights, I suppose, I could have written a liberal book instead of this. I saw Jackie Robinson play for the Brooklyn Dodgers, saw a speech by Martin Luther King, Jr.'s brother, and asked him a question. You have to realize, there were some common purposes in those days between the "conservatives" and the liberals. I used to draw the cover for the student paper of the UW College of Agriculture short course and, in January

1961, I tried to draw a picture of JFK and President Eisenhower shaking hands at the Inauguration, and the caption said, "Thank you Ike and good luck Jack." But that was then and now is now (sigh).

Liberalism has gone to extremes that were nearly unforeseeable. The University of Wisconsin no longer has a baseball team (the team that produced Harvey Kuehn), due to feminist demands on the public coffers. Traditionalists can't even stick a finger in the dike to hold back the tide anymore without being chastised by the politically correct sychophants. If we so much as ask "dumb questions," we are then accused of everything from homophobia to sexism to racism to "trying to impose a theocracy"!

> But rave not thus! and let a Sabbath song
> Go up to God so solemnly the dead may feel no wrong.
> - Edgar Allen Poe (1809-1849)

Say hey, Willie! That would make the best inscription on my Tombstone, and then you can add:

"P.S. There's no crying in baseball, so don't START."

Chapter 3
- The New Media vs. the "Mainstream" news media -

("TRICKLE-DOWN TREASON")

Introduction: "The Scribes"

I WAS INVITED TO ATTEND a UW Badger Herald banquet in the fall of 2004, before the elections. The main speaker was the head of the Mass Communications department of the UW - and it was two days after Dan Rather's "forged documents scandal" had become obvious - I couldn't wait to hear what the good professor was going to say about it. Guess what? He didn't even mention it, but I did overhear him complimenting the editor of the paper for an edition that had attacked the President. I'm afraid that the old conservative Badger Herald has become incestuously "institutionalized" due to the liberal "Mass Communications department."

Curtis Dahlgren

The "Herd Mentality" Of Modern Journalism:

MY father raised sheep. I was around sheep since the day I came home from the hospital. It is a safe assumption that the writers and producers of "Backbroke Mountain" can't say the same, but I've spent 60-some years just observing, and here are some observations from the banks of my memory:

For example, newborn lambs after a week or two show great competitiveness. Lambs will race each other back and forth, forth and back, around the farm yard, each one trying to reach the "turning point" first (as described by Malachi: "You shall go forth and gambol as calves of the stall"). As they mature though, their individuality wanes, and they truly become "SHEEP" in the fullest and most frustrating sense of the word. In other words, they simply "run with the flock."

When the farmer tries to drive them through a gate, as in "to greener pastures," they panic. They run in frenzied circles and semi-circles - anywhere but through the gate. The lambs follow their mothers, and the mothers frantically look for an older sheep to follow, but not one of them has a clue as to where the alpha-sheep is.

Finally, one of them (it could be any one of them) stops running and takes a second look at the gate opening. It immediately does a 40-yard dash through the gate, and the mass confusion converts to a stampede. They all do a 40-yard dash through the gate that they were so resolved to avoid a moment earlier (a perfect example of today's public relations "consensus").

Advertising and public relations experts have probably never seen this phenomenon in their whole lives, but stored somewhere in their genes evidently, there remains an understanding of the sheep instinct of human beings, plus the ability to exploit it. This skill is relatively harmless when it comes to selling soda or cars, but it's no joke when it involves the attempt to reprogram a nation's conscience!

I'm so old that I was conceived before Pearl Harbor, and I miss the days when men were men, the women were glad of it, and the Opposition was "loyal." The "fourth estate," the news media, have become a Fifth Column, and politicians vie with each other for the privilege of stopping oil drilling and gold mining, and the chance to kill the goose that laid the Golden Egg.

> Section 3A:
> "Beware the drama queens in politics and the press"
> www.RenewAmerica.us/columns/dahlgren/060316

"Accuracy is to a newspaper what virtue is to a lady, but a newspaper can always print a retraction."

- Adlai Stevenson

"GOOD NEWS IS NO NEWS." Newspapers seldom print retractions anymore, and they seem to get a perverse pleasure from bad news (whether real or imaginary). Journalists are so arrogant that they think that we are too stupid to catch a "mistake," and that we deserve no apology from them anyway. Like the educators who "taught" them, they have an attitude!

The best way to describe their attitude is to go to an excerpt from one of my early columns: "No more bull" - www.RenewAmerica.us/columns/dahlgren/040319 -

THROUGH A SERENDIPITOUS FLUKE of divine intervention, Abraham Lincoln finds himself resurrected, and instantaneously being interviewed on "60 Minutes" by Andy Rooney. I know that the guy with the combed-over eyebrows doesn't do the interviews, but it makes a great word-picture nonetheless:

Rooney: Mr. President, the first question is, "What took you so long to agree to be interviewed?"

Lincoln: Well, ah, I'm a little foggy about that myself, but I think I was dead.

Rooney: Be that as it may, what the nation really wants to know is, how do you feel about same-sex marriage?

Lincoln: Uh, my ears must have been damaged by the gunshot; I thought you said "same-sex marriage."

Rooney: You heard the question, Mr. President. Do you believe in a Constitutionally guaranteed right to gay marriage?

Lincoln: Well, uh, if that's the question, I suppose Mary and I had a fairly gay marriage. She was a lot gayer than I was though. Some people said that I was WAY too serious!

Rooney: Answer the question, Mr. President. Should people have the right to legally marry someone of their own sex, with a Constitutionally guaranteed right to a marriage license?

Lincoln: Sounds to me as if it has become nothing but a piece of paper!

Rooney: You mean the Constitution or a marriage license?

Lincoln: BOTH. But just for curiosity, what's the next question?

Rooney: The question is, do you believe that a woman has a Constitutionally guaranteed right to an abortion on demand?

Lincoln: Don't tell me; we've fallen under the influence of the Europeans again, haven't we? The next thing you'll be telling me is that we've turned the Panama Canal over to the Chinese, and have left our border with Mexico unguarded.

Rooney: How did you know about the Panama Canal?

Lincoln: That reminds me of a story… [Cut away quickly to a Bob Dole commercial for Viagra. When he hears the words "four hours," Abe has a heart attack and dies again.]

"Let my people go and pray."

Section 3B:
"Sleepless in America"
www.RenewAmerica.us/
columns/dahlgren/040818

"I'm going to Vietnam at the request of the White House. President Johnson says a war isn't really a war without my jokes."

- Bob Hope

THE OTHER NIGHT, I had a dream about an older guy who was reminiscing about the Korean and Vietnam war eras. In the dream, I immediately noticed that his focus was 180 degrees off from my focus. He was focusing on the decline of President Truman's popularity, the end of Senator McCarthy's popularity, the decline of LBJ's popularity, and the resignation of President Nixon. He must have been a retired journalist. He appeared to actually enjoy those potshots. This is called "schadenfreud" - getting pleasure from the suffering of others.

I, on the other hand, was thinking about how sad it was that the firing of MacArthur, and the obsession of the press with the McCarthy story, had made both Truman and Eisenhower less successful than they could have been.

The big story of the 1950s was not Senator McCarthy, but the first war in which America ever settled for a draw. In a war fought under the "United Nations" banner, we settled for a dividing line between the two halves of Korea. After three years and 50,000+ American casualties (and who knows how many POWs) the 48th parallel was actually a few steps backwards from Gen. MacArthur's front lines in the first month or so after his landing in Korea.

Curtis Dahlgren

To many journalists and educators, the "modern era" began during the Vietnam war. Their entire focus is on the fall of President Nixon, with no attention on the fall of Southeast Asia. Oh, we had to watch TV pictures of helicopters leaving the roof of the U.S. embassy in Saigon for 2 or 3 nights, but it was soon over for us, like a temporary hang nail or something. We were so far away that we didn't actually have to care about the fleeing boat people - or the Cambodians dying in the Killing Fields of their "reeducation" camps (or the Hmong hill people we betrayed).

The big story of the 1970s was the first defeat in war suffered by the United States, and a lot of people "enjoyed" that!

AND SO, to bring some perspective to the situation, I wrote an article for the U. of Wisconsin Badger Herald in 1972 entitled "The Strange Saga of the South Dakota Civil War." I reposted it as a column. That article was a rare humor piece on the subject - written from a child-like perspective. It didn't get as much attention as the humor of the Zucker brothers, some of whom were at the UW at the same time. My article was ahead of its time, I suppose, but it went something like this:

"The Strange Saga of the South Dakota 'Civil War'"

ONCE UPON A TIME, long long ago, there was a tiny kingdom far far away called Indo-Dakota. It was so named because it was inhabited by Indians and ruled for many years by the French from the city of Pierre. Following the collapse of the Nationalist government in China, due to "diplomatic" decisions made elsewhere, an underground movement was launched by Bismarck for the purpose of creating an atheistic theocracy in Indo-Dakota.

And so the South was invaded by the North - the Peace Garden State! One day 40,000 Frenchmen found themselves surrounded by gorillas at Dienbienphu, a tiny hamlet on the Missouri River, and the Frenchmen said, "OK, you win" (but not before sending a May Day message to the

"Massey-Harris 101"

District of Columbia requesting at least a token payment on the Statue of Liberty).

"Don't worry, be happy," said the District of Columbia. "An international control commission is going to establish a Demilitarized Zone." And so the State Department sent an ambassador to a Convention in Geneva, which produced the treaty now known as the Louisiana Sellout.

Ten years later, in 1964, an important election was held in the District of Columbia. The challenger, Goldie Bearwater, complained, "North Dakota has been overrunning South Dakota for almost 15 years now; we're going to have to do something about it pretty soon."

"TRIGGER HAPPY!" said the Incumbent. "Elect that guy and he's liable to start a war over there!" Well, the people elected the Incumbent, who stood head and shoulders above every other man in the Kingdom. "I never expected to get so many votes," said he. "Now that we have a CONSENSUS government, ah hereby promise to become all things to all people. For the sake of the 26 million people who voted for that other guy, ah will send 500,000 soldiers to Indo-Dakota. And for the sake of the rest of us, they won't take SIDES in the fighting!"

"Amen for CONSENSUS," said the Congress, in its famous Tonka Truck Resolution (and the Senator from South Dakota offered his blessings, for his wife was a lobbyist for Tonka trucks). Two years later, it became clear to the Incumbent that Tonka trucks just weren't getting the job done, so he sent over two dozen International Scouts, complete with curb feelers mounted on the right front fenders (plus peace feelers to the four corners of the globe).

"About these Scouts with curb feelers, " said the Senator from Arkansas, "Isn't this a drastic escalation of the war?"

"Not at all!" said the Secretary of Defense, Robert S. McNamath. "This is merely an incremental adjustment to meet a new stimulus level."

"Oh," said the Senator from Arkansas. "Oh," said the Senator from South Dakota.

"Balderdash," said a man from Yorba Linda. "Drive it or park it!"

So the Incumbent parked it, and the man from Yorba Linda was elected President. One day he went on television and said, "North Dakota, the Peace Garden State, is stockpiling weapons in Wyoming near the border with South Dakota, so we are going to go in and 'neutralize' those weapons."

There was weeping and gnashing of teeth among the college students at Columbia. "Wyoming has been INVADED," they sobbed. Some of them took it so hard that they tore their Levis and sat down in the ashes of burned-out college buildings throughout the land of Columbia.

Captain Carrey came to comfort them, along with Spock, their baby doc, who suggested very strongly that they should get off their ashes and tear down Columbia (or else he would "thrash them to within an inch of their lives"). A third comforter gave a sensitive speech on the virtues of the Peace Garden State, and then led the children up Pennsylvania Avenue chanting, "Ho Ho Ho, Ho Chi Minh; dare to fight and DARE TO WIN"...

After a while, the man from Yorba Linda went on television again and he said, "At this very hour, the Army of the Republic of South Dakota is on its way to a busy intersection on the Ho Chi Mansfield Highway in Montana, near the border with North and South Dakota, in order to stop the flow of war materials threatening to wipe out Rapid City."

The Senator from South Dakota gave the other party's response, saying:"I do not feel that those Badlands are worth one more penny of the precious resources of Columbia (which could be put to better uses), because those black hills are so far away that they constitute no threat to the security of Washington DC!" And so the Peace Garden State sent three-fourths of its standing army across the Demilitarized Zone, including Russian tanks with volunteers chained to the controls, headed toward the city of Aberdeen.

After a while, the man from Yorba Linda went on TV again, and announced that he was going to mine the harbors of North Dakota and bomb all railroad lines leading to Canada. This time the college students were inconsolable. Anti-war demonstrators were seen marching through the malls chanting, "FIGHT BACK!"

"The NLF is going to win," chanted the Chicago eleven. The Senator from South Dakota was truly moved. A reporter asked him, "Are you prepared to call for an immediate withdrawal of fighting forces?"

"If you mean the forces in Montana, Wyoming, and South Dakota, yes!" he replied. "That is - if you mean OUR forces in Montana, Wyoming, and South Dakota."

Someone suggested that there was still a consensus of opinion that was opposed to unilateral withdrawal. "CONSENSUS IS THE OLD POLITICS," he snorted. "I believe in the NEW politics now."

And so the Senator from South Dakota was nominated to run for President, so let us pray.

[End of article, but not end of story. With so many contemporary journalists rooting for our enemies again, will history be repeated?]

> Behold 'tis the mild idealists who plan our Social Revolutions
> And the brutal realists who turn them into executions;
> And the first ones on their lists are the Mild Idealists.
>
> - poem from the 60s or 70s
(author and title unknown)

"Let my people go and pray."

Section 3C:
"The verboten topics;
or, freedom from Free Speech"

A Few Choice Comments:

"The press is a little like the blackbirds in the fall - one flies off the telephone wire, the others all fly away; and the other one comes back and sits down and they all circle and they all come down and sit… in a row again."

- Senator Eugene McCarthy

"Journalism is a kind of profession, or craft, or racket, for people who never wanted to grow up and go out into the real world. If you're a good journalist, what you do is live a lot of things vicariously, and report them for other people who want to live vicariously."

- Harry Reasoner

"As reporters, we should stay the **** out of politics and maintain a private position on any issue."

- John Chancellor

"There are honest journalists like there are honest politicians. When bought, they stay bought."

- Bill Moyers

"Hitler said that he always knew you could buy the press. What he didn't know was you could get them cheap."

- Mort Sahl

"Journalists were never intended to be the cheerleaders of a society, the conductors of applause, the sycophants. Tragically, that is their assigned role in authoritarian societies, but not here - not yet."

- Chet Huntley [pre-1979]

"Gossip is when you hear something you like about someone you don't."

- Earl Wilson

"Guerrilla journalism came about because we didn't want to be a part of access journalism. We hung out at parties and eavesdropped and stole memos and every other **** thing to crash through."

- Robert Scheer

"I can get a better grasp of what is going on in the world from one good Washington dinner party than from all the background information NBC piles on my desk."

- Barbara Walters

"If a senator is putting his hand on my fanny and telling me how he's going to vote on impeaching President Nixon, I'm not so sure I'm going to remove his hand no matter how demeaning it is."

- Sally Quinn

"Before I refuse to take your questions, I have an opening statement."

- Pres. Reagan

The Outcome That Is Desired By The Media Is More Important To Them Than The Truth As It Exists.

Section 3A was about the attitudes of the news media, and the subject of this one is their intentions ("good intentions" always trump results in the wonderland of journalism, the planet with four moons). John Chancellor's principle, "private positions on any issue," went out of

Curtis Dahlgren

style with the polyester leisure suit. You can't tell the "news" from the "editorial" without a scorecard.

Even before "Are You Smarter Than a Fifth-grader?," the target audience for television was about age 13, the lowest common denominator of the populace. Even National Public Radio, despite a pseudo-intellectual facade, parrots mainly the liberal, immature, side of the coin. As I said in one of my columns:

Ain't relativism and "equality" and self-esteem wonderful? The lowest common denominator rules! We've gone from Camelot to Vunderland in just a few short years. If a member of the audience insists that 2 + 2 = 4, he is put down as a "bigot," and it is explained to him again why 2 + 2 = 5.

"'That's the reason they're called lessons,' the Gryphon remarked: 'because they lesson from day to day'…I only took the regular course… the different branches of Arithmetic - Ambition, Distraction, Uglification, and Derision." It's like another line from "Alice":

"Will you walk a little faster?" said a whiting to a snail. "There's a tortoise close behind us, and he's treading on my tail."

That illustrates the reasons for the popularity of talk radio and Internet news. In the Hinterlands of Kansas or the Upper Peninsula, we don't get invited to those Washington dinner parties, and we also resent being talked down to by the people who do! We want a little coffee with our sugar, more substance than fluff, and the New Media provide the substance. Believe it or not, Babwa, there IS a whole 'nother country out here between the Potomac River and Burbank, California.

> "Is there any other industry in this country which seeks to presume so completely to give the customer what he does not want?"
>
> - Robert Murdoch

Believe it or not, the customer wants to be treated like an adult, but the MSM (mainstream news media) think we can't handle the truth. They would have us remain in "perpetual childhood."

"News" is more about smoke-and-mirrors, 24/7, than mirroring the news. An asteroid could be headed directly for the earth, and the news media would lead off the top of the hour with a "global warming" story or drunken Hollywood floozies, or the latest smoking ban or "smoking gun." Even the mafia has its "standards" and everyone in the world needs at least one thing to hang his "self-esteem" on; for the MSM, its "thing" to feel superior about is pollution - whether caused by smoking or too many people out there exhaling carbon dioxide (I guess).

Politically Incorrect Topics, However, Are Taboo:

-The link between abortion and breast cancer (if women were cows, veterinary medicine probably would have proven the link a long time ago).

- Post-abortion suicide and infertility, and the ability of the baby to feel pain.

-Homosexuals are NOT ten percent of the population [the last honest article on this subject that I recall was in the April 23, 1993 issue of Time magazine (the stat is closer to one percent than ten)].

-"Safe" sex isn't ("gay suicides" and diseases such as MSRA are "covered up" by the MSM).

-If a crime is committed by an illegal alien, the MSM won't even mention the ethnicity of the perpetrator, let alone his legal status.

-The real reasons pro-lifers are pro-life are never mentioned (we are characterized as "women-haters," even though there are more women than men in the pro-life movement).

-Pro-life marches by hundreds of thousands are buried by other news, such as a protest by a handful of so-called "pro-choicers."

-Horrendous crimes committed in the name of Islam or Communism are "minimized" and/or blamed on the United States, our President, or "hopelessness" (never hatred).

-The bias of the news media itself is a verboten topic (we can't even ask dumb questions about that one)!

Years before the term "political correctness" was coined, there appeared a prophetic article entitled "Moral Dishonesty" (National Review, 12/19/75). The author, Gerhart Niemeyer, said in the opening paragraph:

> "A sensational book by the German paleontologist Heinrich Erben maintains that mankind is probably a declining species. He points to certain parallels between extinct animal species that lost their fitness for survival because they were too protected by circumstances, and the human race as it exists today... To Erben's list of human immaturities... let us add another: moral dishonesty."

Niemeyer goes on to say, "In thinking about detente' we tend to see the Soviet regime as a normal government, its relations to its subjects as normal policies [etc]... even though there is much evidence that says, It just ain't so. Evidence disturbing to attitudes of good will toward the Soviet Union is simply read out of court... The truth is conceived as an enemy of international goodness...

> "Self-will may govern our actions but it does not sit easy in our souls. Moral dishonesty, by contrast, not only considers itself guiltless but positively glows in self-righteousness while heaping moral condemnation on those who disagree... Reason takes second place not to traditional morality but to subjective 'moral' intentions and the emotional self-satisfaction of supporting a public cause seen as progressive...

"Traditional morality - either the Ten Commandments, Aristotle's list of virtues, or Christ's double love of God and neighbor - can never pass off falsehood as the necessary price of goodness. That possibility belongs exclusively to modern progressivism... More than Tartuffe, who knew that he was lying, they suppress reason by not allowing the voice of Truth to be heard even within their own hearts. A fraud of secular piety wholly engulfs their being, so that reason is dethroned...

"It goes without saying that in the process not merely reason but morality itself is lost. For where reason and knowledge are despised, there Mephistopheles can easily snare Faust in the net of hell." [my emphasis]

There you have it: the "reason" that modern journalism highlights certain "news" while censoring, suppressing, and outright silencing all opposition is because it makes them "feel good" – and they hate "knowledge" if it's politically incorrect. No wonder "dead-tree" (paper) news isn't selling anymore.

"Let my people go and pray."

Section 3D:
"How the MSM and PR campaigns 'stifle' First Amendment speech"
www.RenewAmerica.us/analyses/051014

"The idea was to create an impression that a mass movement was afoot - that everywhere Congress looked,... everywhere, people were talking about [campaign finance] reform."

- Wayne La Pierre, NRA Executive VP, (on McCain-Feingold")

THE RULE OF THUMB in laying sod is "green side up," but left-wing lawyers, jurists, and politicians have been turning the holy sod of Freedom on its head. The "free exercise of religion" clause of the

Constitution has been replaced with "freedom from religion" and "freedom from free speech."

Too many of our churches sheepishly stand by and watch, while true defenders of Freedom are vilified and blackballed - in a form of "McCarthyism" in reverse. As Congressman Ron Paul says, we the people (including too many Christians) have been "too tolerant, too nice, and too patient" for our own good. Dr. Arthur Voobus was an Estonian who escaped from Communism only to discover a more insidious evil in the Western churches and culture: ambivalence. He had to publish a book privately in 1955 just to try to get the word out, and he quoted then-Ford Foundation executive R.M. Hutchins as follows:

"There must be something wrong with the universal education [that] has made men the victims of charlatans in every field of human activity."

The Awful Truth About "Scampaign Finance Reform":

Like Alice's Wonderland world of euphemisms, catch phrases, and sound bites, the wolves have mastered the art of semantics in order to pull the wool over the eyes of the sheep. The following example is taken from an article in America's 1st Freedom, June 2005, by Wayne La Pierre:

Sean Treglia, a former high-ranking operative of the Pew Charitable Trusts, a foundation worth more than $4 billion, last year openly admitted that passage of the McCain-Feingold campaign finance law - which bans political speech in the 60 days leading up to an election - was engineered, planned, funded, and executed by several lavishly wealthy, anti-gun foundations.

In other words, it was not a grassroots movement of people throughout the country. It was a scam. A fraud. A con job. Or, to be more exact, a midnight assassination hit on America's First Amendment.

In an explosive videotape obtained by the New York Post, Treglia is shown bragging to a conference of professors and so-called "journalists" at the University of Southern California about how he and his co-conspirators completely hoodwinked the U.S. Congress and the American people into buying the 'Bipartisan Campaign Reform Act' atrocity... a jihad by proxy against free speech.

Nearly $140 million was spent to lobby for changes to U.S. campaign laws... 90 percent of the total was spent by just eight foundations. Under the law, charitable foundations may not legally lobby Congress. Instead they grant funding to non-profit groups - groups often ginned up specifically for that purpose - who can spend the money on lobbying.

> "To innovate is not to reform."
> - Edmund Burke

La Pierre continues:

> "One of them was George Soros' 'Open Society Institute,' a primary source of funding for the global gun-ban machine now working with the United Nations to eliminate your Second Amendment Right to Keep and Bear Arms....
>
> "It should be no surprise that the groups pushing bans on free speech would also support gun bans. After all, several members of Congress openly admitted that the whole point of 'campaign reform' was to silence gun owners like you... Jan Schakowsky (D-IL) said [among others], 'If my colleagues care about gun control, then campaign finance is their issue so that the NRA does not call the shots.'"

Thus the scam was a double-reverse 'end around' play aimed at CERTAIN forms of speech including that of the grass roots pro-lifers) - not to get money out of politics (such as George Soro's) - and the scam worked to perfection! La Pierre then states:

"TO SELL THEIR SCHEME to the American public, the press, politicians - and groups behind it - lied about the 'crisis' in American politics and how their law would solve it. In reality, their ban did exactly the opposite: It took the common man out of the political arena. [I would add that in a nation of 300 million people, the 'money in politics' was no more disproportionate than it ever was, but the aim was to take CERTAIN TYPES of 'little people' out of the process by gagging them with double standards.]...

"In other words, the people who are still allowed to speak out in those 60 days [before an election] - the candidates themselves and the national media - have a virtual monopoly on ['free'] speech. Yet multi-billion-dollar foundations responsible for imposing that moratorium on free speech are free to operate as they always have: Setting up subsidiary non-profit groups.... Consider the height of that hypocrisy - and the depth of the duplicity - of the national media, which allowed it to happen without so much as a sound.

"IF ANYONE SHOULD recognize and rally to stop attacks on freedom of speech, you'd expect it to be the national networks, newspapers and so-called mainstream media. After all, whenever anyone questions their abuses of that right, they band together and self-righteously squeal 'First Amendment!'..."

Of course, the "silence of the lambs" (mainstream churches) is equally puzzling, since they have as much to lose as the media in this "reforming" of the First Amendment. Just for the record, I'm for the "little guy" - 5'3" James Madison, whose original draft of the First Amendment read:

> "The civil rights of none shall be abridged on account of religious belief or worship, nor shall any national religion be established, nor shall the full and equal rights of conscience, be in any manner, nor on any pretext, infringed."

What part of "Congress shall make no law restricting Freedom of Speech" does Congress not understand? Elaborating on media silence, La Pierre says,

> "Yet when McCain-Feingold and its 'charitable' cheerleaders in these shadowy organizations attempted to shut down the machinery of political debate in the United States, the media were unaccountably silent. Could it be because the foundations and non-profits pushing campaign 'reform' were wining and dining the media with political hush money? According to New York Post writer Ryan Sager, they've already invested millions in grants to the media... [such as NPR and the Radio and Television News Directors Foundation]."

La Pierre continued:

> "Of course, in the eyes of the media, these contributions didn't add up to chump change when compared to the awesome increase in influence they'd enjoy as soon as campaign 'reform' shut ordinary Americans out of the political process. And really, the distinction doesn't matter: Even if the media weren't completely in cahoots, then they were ignorant and negligent to the point of criminality... You want proof? Go onto the Internet. Do a few searches on Treglia and Pew and 'campaign finance reform' and see how many national news stories you find...

"For proof, just ask the Federal Election Commission, which has been sued by some of these leftist 'pro-reform' groups to begin regulating free political speech on the Internet - and is now under court order to do just that. Indeed, in fact, the FEC already has draft regulations to do so, including:

> "An effective ban on [SOME] online news and commentary web sites [and]... an effective ban on the use of company-owned computer equipment for political communications.

Curtis Dahlgren

So, NPR, Who Is Accusing Whom Of Buying And Selling "Influence"?

"I don't want to hear about it," some of you will say. Isn't rehashing CFR like crying over "spilt milk?" NOT! Mr. La Pierre summarizes his article by saying:

"Bradley Smith, a commissioner of the FEC has warned that, 'It is very likely that the Internet is going to be regulated' under the McCain-Feingold free-speech ban... You can bet that this is only the beginning of a tortuous and tragic journey whose ultimate destination is obvious to anyone who's ever read history." [end of excerpt]

[Note] We are already seeing the results of CFR during the 2008 election campaign. Senator McCain (surprahse, surprahse) was promoted shamelessly by the mainstream media, and many of the voters have been blindly influenced by the "perceptions" the media put out there.

My eyes were opened to the politics of professional public-relations campaigns at a "public hearing" regarding a referendum for a new local high school a few years ago. A local employee of a PR firm donated her services, and a series of "testimonies" were scripted and read at this sham "hearing." At issue was a proposed new high school that would cost a town of 10,000 people 50 million dollars - counting interest. By the end of the evening, the "speakers" had convinced the locals that their taxes not only wouldn't go up, but that the new high school would almost be a "gift" from the state. And they gave the impression that almost no one was against the project.

After the meeting, my brother ran into a couple of guys who had been against the referendum, but they had changed their minds. "I thought you were against it," my brother said.

"We were," they said, "but it sounds like most people want it." They had been hustled, but all they really wanted was to be on the "winning" side. The new high school was built, taxes went up, and I moved out of the state.

I will never forget these examples, some of which relate more to short-term political issues than the long-term principles for which I want this book to be remembered. The bottom line is that despite professional public relations efforts by the loony Left, the good news is that there are still many news-talk radio stations that air "the rest of the story" to the American people. As of early 2008, if you want a second opinion about some issue, you can still get one from talk radio. Kudos to the businesses that sponsor news-talk stations. There was a time when conventional "wisdom" would have discouraged businesses from advertising on a "political" show on radio, or the Internet, but thank God "conventional wisdom" isn't always eternal.

Conventional wisdom at one point was so certain that America would adopt the metric system that the feds started putting kilometers on Interstate highway signs. One reason for a glimmer of HOPE is that the American people just didn't "buy" it. And although the "mainstream" news media isn't out of the loop yet, the New Media keep growing in influence.

No matter who the President is, I "hope" there are still Congressional checks and balances, and "opinionated people" out there who aren't afraid to speak the Truth. Don't laugh, but Spiro T. Agnew uttered some prophetic words about 40 years ago:

> "The day when the network commentators and even the gentlemen of the New York Times enjoyed a form of diplomatic immunity… is over."

> "Let us pray for one extra day of Freedom, and thank the Lord for small favors!"

Chapter 4
- The People of the United States vs. the "Supreme" Court[s] -

("TRICKLE-DOWN DESPOTISM")

Introduction: "The Sadducees"

THE POST-CHRISTIAN ELITISTS HATE THE AMERICAN REVOLUTION. If forced to talk about the Founders, they won't sing any praises. They like to give the impression that our Revolution was orchestrated strictly by rich land-owners and the "wealthy" who used the poor farmers for cannon fodder. Nothing could be further from the truth.

We did have some land-owners involved, but they were mostly home-schooled and self-taught, and they often stood shoulder-to-shoulder with the rest of Washington's army, and the signers of the Declaration of Independence suffered great personal losses for the Cause. The American Revolution was a joint effort by the "rich" and the "poor," and one of the very favorite columns I've ever written was the following one.

Section 4A:
"Tom Paine: Corset maker, bartender, and king breaker"
www.RenewAmerica.us/columns/dahlgren/060809

"These are the times that try men's souls."

-T. Paine

"KING GEORGE III of England eventually went mad. You'd probably go mad too if your mighty army had been defeated by the pen of a corset maker, the likes of Tom Paine."

Now that's the way history should be taught! I wrote that line myself, and it's not overstating the facts, since the American Revolution was the biggest "upset" since David v. Goliath. Paine was a major factor in the American victory, but today most kids have never even heard of him!

Generation XYZ thinks that history began with Elvis, Marilyn, and the Beatles, so let's go back to that little town in Norfolk, England where Thomas Paine was born in 1737. His father was a stay maker (a stay being a strip of whale bone that was used in women's corsets). Young Tom worked in the business (taking measurements). I guess this is one of those "jobs Americans won't do" and led him to migrate to America (just kidding).

Stay making was Paine's trade on and off in his 20s and 30s, but he was never very good at anything (especially not good at handling his money, since he spent a lot of it on books, and got fired twice as an excise tax collector).

After his first wife died in childbirth, he married the daughter of a pub owner, and to make a long story short, the business went belly up. Paine was soon wanted by the debtors' prison (they didn't fool around with deadbeats in those days). To begin the twists in his life's story, Paine had been corresponding with Ben Franklin in London about science.

Paine escaped imprisonment in England twice in his lifetime, thanks once to a letter from Thomas Jefferson, and this time due to a letter of introduction to Franklin's son-in-law in Philadelphia. Paine would later escape the guillotine in France by a miracle, and the dungeon there with the help of future President James Monroe. Paine's lowly jobs and "trials" had miraculously prepared him for his "next life," and here's the amazing "rest of the story":

Imagine; this perennial failure landed in Philly at age 37 with just the letter from Franklin, the shirt on his back, and his pants, plus he was sick with the fever. This homeless Brit's first home in America was as a guest in a doctor's house, an omen that everything was about to change for Paine - and FAST. Had he arrived here in any year other than 1774, we may have never heard of the guy, but here was a guy who thrived on crises, and America was in a crisis. Tom Paine's timing (or that of his guardian angel) was impeccable.

The newspapers in England had been censoring (of course) news from the colonies, so it was only in conversation with Ben Franklin that Paine had learned much about the possible rebellion by the colonies. He was starting from scratch in more ways than one, but with the help of Franklin's letter, Paine soon found himself editing the Pennsylvania magazine - even though he had never written anything professionally in his life!

Within about one year, he published Common Sense, the little pamphlet that would turn the world of King George III upside down. It sold 100,000 copies in three months. It was to the newspapers of the day what talk radio and the Internet are to the mainstream media today: "competition." Within six months, the Declaration of Independence had been signed, and some of Paine's concepts made it into the Declaration itself (not bad "selling" for a bartender who couldn't even sell booze to drunkards in England)!

There is in liberal circles the myth that the American Revolution was just the action of a bunch of aristocrats who, if anything, just "used" the common people for grunts. Not so! Paine's unique perspective - rubbing shoulders with both the common man and the "greats" - enabled him to read all of the people, and to see the shadows of coming events. Outside of Paine and Patrick Henry, not many people in 1774 had thought it realistic to even think about independence from Britain, but Paine knew what was bubbling beneath the surface.

"Common Sense" had changed a lot of hearts and minds, and not with demagoguery but with logic. To the argument that America was "growing" - even under the Crown's thumb - Paine responded:

> "We may as well assert that because a child has thrived upon milk, that it is never to have meat, or that the first twenty years of our lives is to become a precedent for the next twenty years."

He was speaking from experience - and understating it! He was almost 40, and had only been successful for a year or so (and even now he was donating all profits from "Common Sense" to the cause of the Rebellion). Business had never been his bag, but in matters of the big picture out there, his forte was foresight.

He said it wasn't logical that an island across the ocean should forever govern a whole continent when it took 4 or 5 months to communicate back and forth. "We have it in our power," he said, "to begin the world over again. A situation, similar to the present, hath not happened since the days of Noah until now."

Later he said, "So deeply rooted were all the governments of the old world, and so effectually had... tyranny... established itself over the mind, that no beginning could be made in Asia, Africa, or Europe, to reform the political condition of man. Freedom had been hunted around the globe; reason was considered rebellion, and the slavery of fear had made men afraid to think...

> "The sun needs no inscription to distinguish him from darkness, and no sooner did American governments display themselves to the world, than despotism felt a shock, and men began to contemplate redress... The insulted German and the enslaved Spaniard, the Russ and the Pole are beginning to think."

Just before the Declaration of Independence, Paine said, "The birthday of a new world is at hand, and a race of men, perhaps as numerous as all Europe contains, are to receive their portion from the events of a few months."

And The Rest Is "History"!

During the war with England, Paine wrote a series of pamphlets: "Crisis I" (which was read to the troops as they boarded boats to cross the Delaware to fight the Hessians), through Crisis XIII in 1783, at war's end. His concluding remarks included this one:

> "It was the cause of America that made me an author. The force with which it struck my mind, and the dangerous condition the country appeared to me in... made it impossible for me, feeling as I did, to be silent... "

NOTE: Never suppress the urgency of one individual in standing up and speaking out. Never underestimate the power of the pen, and don't get discouraged by "hustling while you wait" for things to happen. Perseverance, they say, is willing to be unhappy for awhile. The bartender from Thetford ended up being an adviser to Presidents, kings, and emperors. The Presidents and Napoleon sought his advice. The Presidents took his advice, but the kings and Napoleon didn't - and look where they ended up: George III in a strait jacket and Napoleon in prison on another island!

Conclusion:
Applying the lessons of Thomas Paine -

Get out your highlighter, or dog-ear this page, because your kids won't hear any of this in school. Our public schools could teach our cultural heritage if they wanted to, but they deliberately don't! Many of the best books in my bookcase are marked "DISCARDED" - purchased for a pittance from various public libraries, and "Tom Paine, Freedom's Apostle," by Leo Gurko is no exception.

I "normally" don't cut deists much slack, but that's one of the lessons of this story. I reluctantly must admit that some deists were closer to the truth than some of the preachers who persecuted Paine viciously in his declining years. His mother had been Church of England and his father was a Quaker, and their squabbles had turned him off to mainstream religion. He was refused burial in a Quaker cemetery, so he was buried on the farm the state of New York had given him as a gift to thank him for his services to America (a farm abandoned by Royalist owners during the war). He had cast his bread upon the waters, and he reaped a righteous return.

In the end, strangely enough, Paine's body was stolen and brought back to England. Why, I don't know, but "the universal man" had returned to the Old World - whether he wanted to or not. While living in France for awhile, he wrote a controversial book, The Age of Reason. He was taken as an atheist after that, and it did have some weaknesses, but he began that book by actually reasserting his belief in a God ["one God"]. As he wrote:

> "I believe that religious duties consist in doing justice, loving mercy [an allusion to Scripture], and endeavoring to make our fellow-creatures happy...
>
> "Some, perhaps, will say: Are we to have no word of God - no revelation? I answer, Yes; there is a word of God; there is revelation. The Word of God is the Creation we behold... It does not depend upon the will of man whether it shall be published or not; it publishes itself from one end of the earth to the other. It preaches to all nations and to all worlds... "

That was enough for him, given his boyhood experiences with religious bickering. Late in life, on account of his perceived "heresy," Paine was abandoned by most American politicians with the exception of James Monroe. Reread the preceding paragraph though; that intro to Age of Reason actually isn't far removed from the words of a great hymn writer, Joseph Addison (1672-1719):

The spacious firmament on high,
With all the blue ethereal sky…
Soon as the evening shades prevail,
The moon takes up the wondrous tale,
And nightly to the listening Earth
Repeats the story of her birth.
Whilst all the stars that round her burn,
And all the planets, in their turn,
Confirm the tidings as they roll,
And spread the truth from pole to pole.
In Reason's ear they all rejoice,
And utter forth a glorious Voice,
For ever singing as they shine,
'The Hand that made us is Divine.'

P.S. Some questions occurred to me when I read about Tom Paine, and one is: If King George III had had the foresight of this uneducated bartender, would he have wasted so many pounds and so many soldiers on a futility?

If Napoleon had had the foresight of this corset maker, would he have gone ahead and wasted the lives of 10 million Europeans?

If the Confederates had had the foresight of this tract writer, and known the outcome (half a million deaths), would they still have gone ahead with their hot-headed little revolution? [Note: the South just "loved it" when Federal power trumped the states - when the Feds were retrieving runaway slaves.]

If Hitler were rational and knew that his little jaunt into a neighboring country would inevitably lead to the deaths of 50 million people worldwide, would he do it again?

In the latter's case at least, the answer is yes; like the proverbial scorpion, that's what evil men do, and the NEXT world war could kill billions, not millions!

Curtis Dahlgren

As in 1930s Germany, the winds of "change" are blowing and I have to wonder how long America can survive like this (when political correctness "rules"). As David wrote:

> "Horror hath taken hold upon me because of the wicked who forsake Thy Law."

There are times when wisdom is 9/10 discretion, and other times when it is 9/10 guts. I wonder if a modern-day President would have the guts - with the ACLU looking over his shoulder - to issue the following Proclamation:

> "Whereas a joint Committee of both Houses of Congress has waited on the President of the United States, and requested him to recommend a day of public humiliation, prayer and fasting, to be observed by the people of the United States...
>
> "And whereas it is fit and becoming in all people, at all times, to acknowledge and revere the Supreme Government of God; to bow in humble submission to His chastisements; to confess and deplore their sins and transgressions in the full conviction that the fear of the Lord is the beginning of wisdom...
>
> "And whereas, when our own beloved Country, once, by the blessing of God, united, prosperous and happy, is now afflicted with faction and... war, it is peculiarly fit for us to recognize the hand of God in this terrible visitation, and in sorrowful remembrance of our own faults and crimes as a nation and as individuals, to humble ourselves before Him, and to pray for His mercy, - to pray that we may be spared further punishment, though justly deserved..."

-signed, Abraham Lincoln,
this 12th day of August A.D. 1861

My copy of that Proclamation was sent to me by a friend named Rich, nine days after 9/11, 2001. Rich is dead now, gunned down by another friend of mine who lost his sanity in 2005, but in his e-mail, Rich noted that Lincoln chose September 26, 1861 for that day of fasting. Rich said,

"It is interesting to note that Thursday, September 26, 1861 was Tishri 22, the Last Great Day of the Feast that year."

[Sidebar: With our educrats teaching our kids about Islamic Holy Days, how come they never mention the Feast of Tabernacles or Pentecost? I don't sense much "diversity" there, do you?]

However unlikely it is that a President today would issue such a Proclamation, sometimes, I still see glimmers of hope. I attended a local parade [in 2006] and I believe three bands played the "Battle Hymn" of the Republic. One float had a soloist singing "God Bless America" - for the entire length of the parade route - right out there in the open air of the public square! God is indeed "sifting out the hearts of men before His judgment seat" and Truth is MARCHING!

America has come full circle: We are once again seeing a struggle between the common people of the grass roots versus the elitists and atheists who won't take advice from "bartenders" or pamphleteers. This isn't your father's Republican or Democratic parties anymore, nor Thomas Paine's America. This isn't the "Age of Reason" that he had in mind. As he said:

"The Word of God is the Creation we behold [and furthermore] It publishes itself from one end of the earth to the other. It preaches to all nations and to all worlds... "

That bears repetition. Besides that, he and his colleagues in the Revolution preached limits on human governments (as opposed to the "Supreme Government of God" of Lincoln).

"*Now what, America?*":

There was a fork in the road for America in 1905. After years of decline by the "mainstream" churches, there was a token revival in many cities across the land. The Denver Post of January 20, 1905 reported on the event, typical of many on that day:

"The marts of trade were deserted between noon and two o'clock this afternoon and all worldly affairs were forgotten, and the entire city was given over to meditation of higher things... Going to and and coming from the great meetings, the thousands of men and women radiated this Spirit which filled them, and the clear Colorado sunshine was made brighter by the reflected glow of the light of God shining from happy faces. Seldom has such a remarkable sight been witnessed - an entire great city, in the middle of a busy weekday, bowing before the throne of heaven and asking and receiving the blessings of the King of the Universe."

Even after the Columbine and Colorado Springs massacres, there has been no repeating of even two hours of such public penitence, let alone an official day of prayer. Why not, I wonder? Instead, we have "seminars" on atheism, "trumpeted" by the Press. Why?

My father was only four years old in 1905, but another wise man I once met was old enough to remember the "Spirit of the Age." He wrote that in those days one could hear farmers walking behind their plows singing at the top of their lungs, or whistling merrily. Most people have never even heard of whistling anymore. There's a lot of angst in Mudville today. Casey is down to his last strike.

While a remnant of the 1905 revival remains in spirit, the professors who followed in the footsteps of Wilson have hijacked America. In 1905, one-fourth of the students at Yale went to prayer meetings and Bible studies. But not anymore! This would be a good time for writing "Crisis - #14."

Section 4B:
"Will the Real Thomas Jefferson
please stand up?"
www.RenewAmerica.us/columns/
dahlgren/040128 [excerpted and updated]

"We hold these Truths to be self-evident... "

THIS IS THE PRESIDENT'S' DAY WEEKEND 2008. The other day on my way back from town, I was imagining what a high school "language" teacher (English isn't even the "official" language of "English" classes anymore) would do today if she had to grade Thomas Jefferson's writing. She would probably give the Declaration of Independence a D- or an F for excessive use of capital letters, antiquated language, and long sentences (I said to myself). Come to find out, Jon Sanders posted a column on the same subject, the same day, at www.TownHall.com (2/15/08).

Sanders reported that a member of the Democrat party sent an e-mail (real or imagined I don't know), to a political consultant for one of the "democratic" Presidential candidates. This e-mail consisted of the complete text of the Declaration, under the Subject line "Remember, a top Democrat wrote this." In a very believable scenario, Sanders says that the politico mistook it for a speech writer's suggestion for a major address by his candidate, and the sender received a reply with some very harsh comments. Here's an excerpt from Sanders' column, "A Declaration in Dependence" (the first paragraph is Thomas Jefferson's):

But when a long train of abuses and usurpations, pursuing invariably the same Object evinces a design to reduce them under absolute Despotism, it is their right, it is their duty, to throw off such Government, and to provide new Guards for their future security.

Comment: "Huh?"

Suggestion: And right now, we are all frogs sitting in boiling water. And we need to jump out with hope and dreams and reach for the change we need. This is for the future. This is for the children. This is for the planet itself.
I'm not reading any further. What you have written is way too long, too speechy, and too fundy- christianity. In glancing over the rest, it seems you've listed several dozen policy disputes. That's the wrong approach. Don't forget all the single-issue voters out there. You don't want to scare off a possible supporter based on one political difference. The more policy positions you take, the greater this risk.

Remember the KISS principle: Keep it simple, stupid. Don't do anything to stop the voter from feeling that your candidate agrees with him. Elections aren't about policies, they're about feeling safe and happy.

Oh, and don't forget to end with "Sí, se puede! Yes, we can!" The focus groups are eating that up right now.

End of excerpt. On March 4, 2008 the USA Today published an article by Jonah Goldberg in which he suggests that citizens ought to refuse to talk to pollsters anymore. This would force politicians to run on their honest beliefs rather than on what they think people want to hear. He says, "Without knowing who was in the lead until votes were actually cast, candidates might actually campaign on conviction."

"History is more or less bunk."

- Henry Ford

Let's play "What's My Line?" Contestant #1 says, "My name is Tom Jefferson and I was a Deist."

Contestant #2 says, "My name is Tom Jefferson and I was a secular philosopher of the Enlightenment."

Contestant #3 says, "My name is Tom Jefferson and I was a pioneer lawyer in the Freedom from religion movement."

Our panel of "experts" says: "All of the above!"

SURVEY SEZ: "The 'experts' must know what they're talking about, right?" But would "You Bet Your Life," or even your De Soto, on that? GONG! Better NOT!

The magic word for the day is bunkum; say the magic word and you get a gold star. The "Jefferson" described above is a fictional character who never existed. Our friendly local purveyors of social "science" have swallowed a line - hook, bait, and bobber. But who WAS the real Thomas Jefferson?

The awkward "trivia" fact for those who teach our teachers is: Jefferson left behind 18,000 public and private letters that we know of, plus his official speeches and papers. With all that evidence, how could so many, for so long, be so wrong? I hate to have to be the one to burst the bubble, but here's just a small sample of Jefferson's actions as President of the United States:

-He attended religious services in the Capitol Building (and such services were also held in the Supreme Court building)!

-He favored using the word "God" in the national motto!

-He granted land, buildings, and salaries for clergy teaching in Indian schools!

-Supported the use of the Bible as reading materials in such schools!

-He personally prayed at public events!

-Exempted churches from taxation!

In 1801, he wrote that "the Christian religion, when divested of the rags in which [the clergy] have enveloped it, is a religion of all others most friendly to liberty, science, and freest expansion of the human mind."

Sorry about that, Annie. The freedom from religion foundations and ACLU keep bouncing back and forth between saying it is impossible to know the original intent of the Founders, but then quoting them when such quotes can be twisted to appear to support their agenda. On the one hand, they and their lawyers, with the support of the news media, use early Jeffersonian quotes - and quotes from his enemies during his political campaigns - while trying to keep a lid on later Jefferson thoughts with the other hand.

Certainly he read philosophers such as Plato (he read everything, but he didn't like Plato). But he also read the Bible in four languages! He

Curtis Dahlgren

was 33 years old when he wrote the Declaration of Independence, and over the next 50 years (it should go without saying) his view of the universe had "evolved" and had been fine-tuned! After losing a wife and daughter, and approaching the end of his own life, his letters - especially to John Adams, took on a "new tone."

One of his biographers, who spent over 50 years studying Jefferson the man, said that when he was young he thought he would someday know Jefferson completely - but that in the end, he didn't think anyone in this life would ever really know Jefferson. That makes it all the more outrageous when latter-day "historians" dogmatically claim to "know" that he was a Deist or an advocate of absolute "separation" of religion and from the public square!

Deists believed in a hands-off God, a world without miracles; Jefferson thought America was a miracle! Most of the clergy called him an infidel when he ran for President (mainly over the Trinity doctrine, on which my own views are closer to Jefferson's than to the clergymen). Anyway, he would be dumbfounded to wake up and discover that ONE out of his 18,000 letters is now being used to try to "cleanse" the public square, and the arena of ideas, of religion (that Virginia's Freedom OF Religion is now "Freedom FROM Religion")!

Jefferson had us pegged from the beginning though. As were the rest of the Founders, he was realistic about human nature, and once said that "from the conclusion of this [Revolutionary] war, we will be going downhill." To the orthodox Left, virtue is repulsive, so one's "self-esteem" can only be enhanced by poking holes in the armor of our heroes, with shoddy and very shallow scholarship.

In "the olden days," even orphans had a role model, the "Father of our country." Those of us who went to the "old school" always knew that Washington was a virtuous man with or without the "cherry tree" story. The evidence was there, but the New Age schools are using the cherry tree story as the excuse to toss out 22 million volumes of evidence about our forebears from the Library of Congress (figuratively speaking)! And some of those schools that were named for Washington have even changed their names; it's all about the "true" agenda!

There will be consequences for this wild joy ride by our educators. Lincoln once said that those who twist history have "no right to mislead others, who have less access to history, and less leisure to study it, into [a] false belief... " Teddy Roosevelt also has a quote about those who intentionally mislead others in the name of obtaining "leadership" during a political campaign. Today, people have been grossly misled about "separation of church and state."

Speaking of evidence, here's Item #1: In 1777, the stock of Bibles was dwindling in America due to Britain's trade embargo, and a committee of the Continental Congress said that "the use of the Bible is so universal and its importance so great that your committee refer the above to the consideration of Congress, and if Congress shall not think it expedient to order the importation of types and paper, the Committee recommend that Congress... import 20,000 Bibles form Holland, Scotland, or elsewhere...

"Whereupon it was resolved accordingly to direct said Committee to import 20,000 copies of the Bible." [quoted from The Rebirth of America, by the De Moss Foundation]

In 1781, the publisher of The Pennsylvania Magazine petitioned Congress for money for printing more Bibles - and Congress approved the proposal. You won't hear such facts in the public schools anymore, unless the People demand "Truth in Education"!

John Adams' last words were, "Jefferson still lives." He didn't know that Jefferson had died earlier on the same day, July 4, 1826, but his words are prophetic. Lincoln said that "soberly, it is now no child's play to save the principles of Jefferson from total overthrow in this nation"! The same is true today, and this isn't just an "intellectual jousting match" among eggheads, nor a game that politicians and judges ought to play. There are consequences out in the real world, intended or not intended!

Curtis Dahlgren

As I said, boys and girls, the word for the day is "bunkum." Back in the 1820s, there was a congressman from Buncombe County, North Carolina and one day he gave an extremely long and boring, meaningless to the business at hand, speech in Congress. He explained to friends later that he had only been "speaking to Buncombe." Thus originated Henry Ford's term, bunk (short for "Buncombe").

In the "soft sciences" in our colleges and universities today, much of what passes for wisdom is just subjective bunk aimed at pleasing one's professor and/or graduate teacher, who in turn is just trying to please his department head, who may be just trying to please some new theory out there in the pop culture (i.e., Buncombe). And in politics, not much has "changed."

"You can't fight city hall," they used to say. Now we are told that it's impossible to fight political correctness – AND THE PEOPLE ARE GETTING WEARY OF THIS!

It's time for Tom Paine's "Crisis #14."

Section 4C:
"Jefferson's first inaugural address, RMV (Revised Modern Version)"
www.RenewAmerica.us/columns/dahlgren/070106

"A man sufficiently gifted with humor is in small danger of succumbing to flattering delusions about himself, because he cannot help perceiving what a pompous ass he would become if he did."

- Konrad Lorenz

TRY TO IMAGINE THE INAUGURAL ADDRESS AT SOME FUTURE DATE - at the inauguration of a candidate who was acceptable to the news and entertainment media - a man who is sort of a cross between Rocky Balboa and a "Rock star." The following is the way I envision his inaugural address, using the words of Jefferson contrasted with the "trash talking" of Hollywood's "ideal" candidate:

Friends and Fellow-Citizens:

Dudes!

Called upon to undertake the duties of the first executive office of our country, I avail myself of the presence of that portion of my fellow-citizens which is here assembled to express my grateful thanks for the favor with which they have been pleased to look toward me, to declare a sincere consciousness that the task is above my talents, and that I approach it with those anxious and awful presentiments which the greatness of the charge and the weakness of my powers so justly inspire.

Yo! Whazzup?

A rising nation, spread over a wide and fruitful land, traversing all the seas with the rich productions of their industry, engaged in commerce with nations who feel power and forget right, advancing rapidly to destinies beyond the reach of mortal eye - when I contemplate these transcendent objects, and see the honor, the happiness, and the hopes of this beloved country committed to the issue and auspices of this day, I shrink from the contemplation, and humble myself before the magnitude of the undertaking.

Can you dig it? Today's da day!

Utterly, indeed, should I despair did not the presence of many whom I here see remind me that in the other high authorities provided by our Constitution I shall find resources of wisdom, of virtue, and of zeal on which to rely under all difficulties. To you, then, gentlemen, who are charged with the sovereign functions of legislation, and to those associated with you, I look with encouragement for that guidance and support which may enable us to steer with safety the vessel in which we are all embarked amidst the conflicting elements of a troubled world.

Curtis Dahlgren

Y'all - let's do lunch some time!

During the contest of opinion through which we have passed the animation of discussions and of exertions has sometimes worn an aspect which might impose on strangers unused to think freely and to speak and to write what they think; but this being now decided by the voice of the nation, announced according to the rules of the Constitution, all will, of course, arrange themselves under the will of the law, and unite in common efforts for the common good. All, too, will bear in mind this sacred principle, that though the will of the majority is in all cases to prevail, that will... must be reasonable; that the minority possess their equal rights, which equal law must protect, and to violate would be oppression.

Hey - tonight's da night we rule! [standing ovation]

Let us, then, fellow-citizens, unite with one heart and one mind. Let us restore to social intercourse that harmony and affection without which liberty and even life itself are but dreary things. And let us reflect that, having banished from our land that religious intolerance under which mankind so long bled and suffered, we have yet gained little if we countenance a political intolerance as despotic, as wicked, and capable of as bitter and bloody persecutions.

So just chill out, okay? [delirious standing ovation]

During the throes and convulsions of the ancient world, during the agonizing spasms of infuriated man, seeking through blood and slaughter his long-lost liberty, it was not wonderful that the agitation of the billows should reach even this distant and peaceful shore; that this should be more felt and feared by some and less by others, should divide opinions as to measures of safety. But every difference of opinion is not a difference of principle. We have called by different names brethren of the same principle. We are all Republicans, we are all Federalists...

Just live and let live! We're gonna live high on the hog now. Two chickens in every pot! Maybe two pots for every chicken! And pot's now legal! [standing-O]

"Massey-Harris 101"

I know, indeed, that some honest men fear that a republican government can not be strong, that this Government is not strong enough... I believe this, on the contrary, the strongest Government on earth. I believe it the only one where every man, at the call of the law, would fly to the standard of the law, and would meet invasions of the public order as his own personal concern.

And long live illegal immigration! Si,se puede! [standing ovation]

Sometimes it is said that man can not be trusted with the government of himself. Can he, then, be trusted with the government of others? Or have we found angels in the forms of kings to govern him? Let history answer this question.

And remember - I mean, like - I be da MAN now! [another standing ovation]

Let us, then... possessing a chosen country, with room enough for our descendants to the thousandth and thousandth generation... Acknowledging and adoring an overruling Providence, which by all its dispensation proves that it delights in the happiness of man here and his greater happiness hereafter -

God, I could use a beer about now! [even longer standing ovation]

With all these blessings, what more is necessary to make us a happy and a prosperous people? Still one thing more, fellow-citizens - a wise and frugal Government, which shall restrain men from injuring one another, shall leave them otherwise free to regulate their own pursuits of industry and improvement, and shall not take from the mouth of labor the bread it has earned.

Feel free to ask what da gov'ment can do for you! Free health insurance and free beer for everyone! [thunderous ovation]

It is proper you should understand what I deem the essential principles of our Government, and consequently those which ought to

Curtis Dahlgren

shape its Administration. I will compress them within the narrowest compass they will bear, stating the general principle, but not all its limitations... Equal and exact justice to all men, of whatever state or persuasion, religious or political...Freedom of religion; freedom of the press, and freedom of person under protection of the habeas corpus, and trials by juries impartially selected. These principles form the bright constellation which has gone before us and guided our steps through an age of revolution and reformation. The wisdom of our sages and blood of our heroes have been devoted to their attainment. They should be the creed of our political faith, the text of civic instruction, the touchstone by which to try the services of those we trust...

> No mo home-schoolin'. Safe sex for EVERYONE! [the usual standing-0]

Relying, then, on the patronage of your good will, I advance with obedience to the work, ready to retire from it whenever you become sensible how much better choice it is in your power to make. AND MAY THAT INFINITE POWER WHICH RULES THE DESTINIES OF THE UNIVERSE LEAD OUR COUNCILS TO WHAT IS BEST, AND GIVE THEM A FAVORABLE ISSUE FOR YOUR PEACE AND PROSPERITY.

> GOD-AWESOME! AND NOW - AWW-RRRIGHT! IT'S TIME TO P-A-R-T-Y!! [crowd chants "Si, Si, Si" and proceeds to trash the Capitol Building and the National Cathedral.]

P.S. Yogi Berra said, "There is nothing harder to predict than the future." I hope this column wasn't a foretaste of our future, but - based on recent trends – I wouldn't bet against it either.

It's time for Tom Paine to write "Crisis #14."

Section 4D:
"Politicians vs. the Constitution:
A fistful of words"

"The illegal we do immediately. The unconstitutional takes a little longer."

- Henry Kissinger

Here Are Some Good Quotations Today's Politicians Should Read:

"Don't be humble; you're not that great."

- Golda Meir

"A lot of congressmen and senators like to draw their breath and their salaries and not do much else."

- Sam Ervin

"All of us in the Senate live in an iron lung - the iron lung of politics - and it is no easy task to emerge from that rarified atmosphere in order to breathe the same fresh air our constituents breathe."

- John F. Kennedy

"We were always subject to this pressure from the cause people. We reacted to every threat from women, or militants, or college groups. If I had to do it all over again, I'd learn to tell them to go to hell."

- Frank Mankiewitz (George McGovern's presidential campaign director)

"A liberal is a man too broadminded to take his own side in a quarrel."

- Robert Frost

"The function of liberal Republicans is to shoot the wounded after battle."

- Eugene McCarthy

"Sometimes I think this country would be better off if we could just saw off the eastern seaboard and let it float out to sea."

- Barry Goldwater

"The difference between the men and the boys in politics is, and always has been, that the boys want to be something, while the men want to do something."

- Eric Sevareid

"The evolutionary process in governments continues. We have passed from Feudalism to Capitalism. Our current stage, as we all know, is corruption."

- Jules Feiffer

"The accomplice to the crime of corruption is frequently our own indifference."

- Bess Myerson

"The function of socialism is to raise suffering to a higher level."

- Norman Mailer

"The only place socialism works is in heaven, where they don't need it, and in hell, where they already have it."

- Ronald Reagan

"Politics does not make strange bedfellows; it only seems that way to those who have not been following the courtship."

- Kirkpatrick Sale

"How can anyone govern a nation that has 240 different kinds of cheese?"

- Charles de Gaulle

"Diplomacy, like politics, is the art of the possible; and if we use our leverage toward an unachievable end, we will create a mess."

- George W. Ball

"In Israel, in order to be a realist, you must believe in miracles."

- David Ben-Gurion

"It is when all play safe that we create a world of utmost insecurity."

- Dag Hammarskjold

"Cowardice asks the question - is it safe? Vanity asks the question - is it popular?... But conscience asks the question - is it right? There comes a time when one must take a position that is neither safe, popular, or political, but because it is right."

- Martin Luther King, Jr.
[from "The Book of Quotes" by Barbara Rowes, Ballantine, 1979]

OBVIOUSLY, the challenge for our leaders today is being able to tell the difference between what is right and "unpopular" and something that is wrong but too popular (in other words, knowing when to listen to the people and when not to). Listening to the people takes guts, but a modest rule of thumb would be to say that politicians ought to listen to the people a lot more than they do!

Francis Bacon said, "The voice of the people hath some divineness in it, else how should so many men agree to be of one mind?"

David Crosby said, "I don't think politics is a workable system any more... They gotta invent something better." [such as what?]

As Drew Pearson said, "Government is only as good as the men in it." That's scary, because most people in government don't realize that the New York Times isn't the Voice of the People.

P.S. Here are a few more lines from Edmund Burke (1729-1797):

> "It is a general popular error to imagine the loudest complainers for the public to be the most anxious for its welfare."
> "Because half a dozen grasshoppers under a fern make the field ring with their importunate chink, whilst thousands of great cattle, reposed beneath the shadow of the British oak, chew the cud and are silent, pray do not imagine that those who make the noise are the only inhabitants of the field... "
> "There is but one law for all, namely, that law which governs all, the law of our Creator, the law of humanity, justice, equity - the law of nature and of nations."
> "It is not what a lawyer tells me I may do; but what humanity, reason, and justice, tell me I ought to do."
> "Falsehood has a perennial spring."
> "Corrupt influence, which is itself the perennial spring of all prodigality, and of all disorder; which loads us more than millions of debt; which takes away vigor from our arms, wisdom from our councils, and every shadow of authority and credit from the most venerable parts of our constitution... "

If Burke sounds more like a Colonist than a Redcoat, that's because our Founders were fighting more for Independence as a Nation than for independence from traditional conservative English thinking.

Those educators who look "backward" only in order to rewrite history would like you to believe that the French philosophers and revolutionaries were the models for the American Revolution. Nothing could be further from the truth. The Hebrew Bible and English philosophers were much more quoted by our Founding Fathers (studies have proven).

Edmund Burke achieved immortality, fame-wise, in spite of a lackluster academic career. As the Encyclopedia Britannica (11th edition) says, "It is too often the case to be a mere accident that men who become eminent for wide compass of understanding and penetrating comprehension, are in their adolescence unsettled and desultory."

So the word-for-the-day, boys and girls, is "desultory"! My trusty 38 Funk & Wagnalls says that desultory means "passing abruptly and irregularly from one thing to another; exhibiting or resulting from unsystematic or disconnected effort or application: fitful; changeable; as, desultory study, reading, conversation, or remarks."

Just think, they could have put him on Ritalin because he "couldn't focus."

Many great men including Einstein started out in life as "restless" students. The historian Edward Gibbon (1737-1794) said:

> "To the University of Oxford I acknowledge no obligation; and she will as cheerfully renounce me for a son, as I am willing to disclaim her for a mother. I spent fourteen months at Magdalen College: they proved the fourteen months the most idle and unprofitable of my whole life."

There's another "uncredentialed" scholar who became a Member of Parliament and left behind a few words of advice for politicians ("The Decline and Fall of the Roman Empire"). He himself was given eight pages of fine print in the Encyclopedia Britannica, 11th edition, but how many "scholars" today have even heard of "The Decline and Fall," let alone having read it?

America may not be long for this world - unless America can turn around its educational and political philosophies. I wish Tom Paine could start writing "Crisis #14."

Section 4E:
"A few words more: An open letter to the
Judicial and political class"
www.RenewAmerica.us/
columns/dahlgren/070816

"In a time of universal deceit - telling the truth is a revolutionary act."

- George Orwell

BY GOING TO www.brainyquotes.com and reading a few Orwell quotes, I came to realize that he was even greater as a writer than I had understood. Today's colleges probably ignore his writings or quote him out of context. Orwell was briefly intrigued by British Socialism, but quickly saw it for what it was – sort of a "rebel without a cause" - so, Orwell isn't as "popular" as he once was (and he was too much of a "prophet" to have much honor among his own people).

Let's Go To The Horse's Mouth (George Orwell) For A Few Quotations:

There are some ideas so wrong that only a very intelligent person could believe in them.

We have now sunk to a depth at which restatement of the obvious is the first duty of intelligent men.

What can you do against the lunatic who is more intelligent than yourself, who gives your arguments a fair hearing and then simply persists in his lunacy?

The great enemy of clear language is insincerity. When there is a gap between one's real and one's declared aims, one turns, as it were, instinctively to long words and exhausted idioms, like a cuttlefish squirting out ink.

But if thought corrupts language, language can also corrupt thought.

He was an embittered atheist, the sort of atheist who does not so much disbelieve in God as personally dislike Him.

Enlightened people seldom or never possess a sense of responsibility.

Progress and reaction have both turned out to be swindles.

All political thinking for years past has been vitiated in the same way. People can foresee the future only when it coincides with their own wishes, and the most grossly obvious facts can be ignored when they are unwelcome.

If liberty means anything at all, it means the right to tell people what they do not want to hear.

In our age there is no such thing as 'keeping out of politics.' All issues are political issues, and politics itself is a mass of lies, evasions, folly, hatred and schizophrenia.

Doublethink means the power of holding two contradictory beliefs in one's mind simultaneously, and accepting both of them.

The very concept of objective truth is fading out of the world. Lies will pass into history.

Who controls the past controls the future. Who controls the present controls the past.

Curtis Dahlgren

Early in life I had noticed that no event is ever correctly reported in a newspaper.

In our time political speech and writing are largely the defense of the indefensible.

Liberal: a power worshiper without power.

No advance in wealth, no softening of manners, no reform or revolution has ever brought human equality a millimeter nearer.

One does not establish a dictatorship in order to safeguard a revolution; one makes a revolution in order to establish a dictatorship.

Political language... is designed to make lies sound truthful and murder respectable, and to give an appearance of solidity to pure wind.

The atom bombs are piling up in the factories, the police are prowling through the cities, the lies are streaming from the loudspeakers, but the earth is still going round the sun.

A family with the wrong members in control; that, perhaps, is as near as one can come to describing England in a phrase.

As with the Christian religion, the worst advertisement for Socialism is its adherents.

"Got Solutions?"
[Orwell Also Said The Following.]

Men can only be happy when they do not assume that the object of life is happiness.

To survive it is often necessary to fight and to fight you have to dirty yourself.

I sometimes think that the price of liberty is not so much eternal vigilance as eternal dirt.

Language ought to be the joint creation of poets and manual workers.

Political chaos is connected with the decay of language... one can probably bring about some improvement by starting at the verbal end.

Freedom is the freedom to say that two plus two make four. If that is granted, all else follows.

We sleep safe in our beds because rough men stand ready in the night to visit violence on those who would do us harm.

War is war... There is hardly such a thing as a war in which it makes no difference who wins.

A tragic situation exists precisely when virtue does not triumph but when it is still felt that man is nobler than the forces which destroy him.

Conclusion:

I'm not going to explain what Orwell meant by those sayings line-by-line (that's what we taxpayers hire college professors and/or illegal aliens to do for you). I figure this book has a better shot at immortality if it will provide employment to those who always ask the question (without necessarily answering it), "What did this writer mean by that?" Given the Left wing's lack of humor, this book is chock full of things the lefties won't "get." Here are a few more quickies from Orwell:

The aim of a joke is not to degrade the human being, but to remind him that he is already degraded.

At fifty everyone has the face he deserves.

Curtis Dahlgren

Advertising is the rattling of a stick inside a swill bucket.

If you have embraced a creed which appears to be free from the ordinary dirtiness of politics – a creed from which you yourself cannot expect to draw any material advantage – surely that proves that you are in the right?

The implication there is that that's ludicrous! Just because you imagine yourself to be serving a "noble" cause, well – it ain't necessarily so! Both the religious and secular Pharisees ought to take warning from those words. Orwell was a "prophet" in the sense that he had a heightened sense of observation, as in

> "What is wrong with this picture?"

Orwell also said, "Society has always seemed to demand a little more from human beings than it will get in practice."

P.S. The most maddening thing about that is, the same people who tend to say "all politicians are crooks" are the same people who want politicians to micromanage our local affairs and personal lives from far-off Washington DC (and the people who were first in line to promote the sexual revolution of the 60s and 70s are the same people who now act like fascists and "thought police" on selected issues). www.RenewAmerica.us/columns/dahlgren/030909

It's time for a "Crisis #14" by a Tom Paine.

Section 4F:
"Politicians vs. the People:
Another fistful of words"
www.RenewAmerica.us/
columns/dahlgren/071130

"Vanity of vanities, saith the preacher; all is vanity. He still taught the people knowledge, and set in order many proverbs."

- Solomon (977 B.C.?)

"Massey-Harris 101"

[Rather than railing on the Establishment with my own words, here are some words of wisdom from the 16th and 17th century. For those ladies at Harvard or MIT who aren't good at math and may be getting short of breath, that means more than 400 years ago. They were written by a home-schooled boy who became an adviser to the English crown.]

"Books will speak plain when counselors blanche."

THERE BE [SOME WHO] CAN PACK THE CARDS AND YET CANNOT PLAY WELL; so there are some that are good in canvasses and factions, that are otherwise weak men.

Every rod and staff of empire is truly crooked at the top.

Universities incline wits to sophistry and affectation.

For what a man had [wished to] be true he more readily believes.

There is more of the fool in human nature than of the wise.

Laws are like cobwebs; where the small flies are caught, and the great break through.

Nothing doth more hurt in a state than when the cunning men pass for wise.

He said it that knew it best.

Intermingle earnest with jest.

Envy never takes a holiday.

A wise man will make more opportunities than he finds.

Fortunes… come tumbling into some men's laps.

In the youth of a state arms do flourish; in the middle age of a state, learning; and then both of them for a time; in the declining age of a state, mechanical arts and merchandise.

Suspicions amongst thoughts are like bats amongst birds, they ever fly at twilight.

There is nothing makes a man suspect much, more than to know little.

The inquiry of truth, which is the love-making, or wooing of it, the knowledge of truth, which is the presence of it, and the belief of truth, which is the enjoying of it, is the sovereign good of human nature.

What is truth? said jesting Pilate; and would not stay for an answer.

A man that studieth revenge keeps his own wounds green.

It were better to have no opinion of God at all than such an opinion as is unworthy of Him; for the one is unbelief, the other is contumely [an ostentatious display of contempt].

There is a superstition in avoiding superstition.

They that deny God destroy men's nobility.

A little philosophy inclineth men's mind to atheism, but depth in philosophy bringeth men's minds about to religion.

God never wrought miracle to convince atheism, because His ordinary works convince it.

There was never a miracle wrought by God to convert an atheist, because the light of nature might have led him to confess a God.

I had rather believe all the fables in the legend, and the Talmud, and the Alcoran, than that this [universe] is without a mind.

Silence is the virtue of fools.

All colours will agree in the dark.

It is true greatness to have in one the frailty of a man, and the security of a God.

The pencil of the Holy [Spirit] hath laboured more in describing the afflictions of Job than the felicities of Solomon.

Prosperity is the blessing of the Old Testament, adversity is the blessing of the New.

Prosperity doth best discover vice, but adversity doth best discover virtue.

Riches are a good handmaid, but the worst mistress.

- Francis Bacon (Baron Verulam, Viscount St. Albans, 1561-1626)

[Another college dropout whose life and works nonetheless earned him more than 16 pages in the Encyclopedia Britannica, 11th edition - which described him as 'the great leader in the reformation of modern science and philosophy':

"The time was ripe for a great change; scholasticism, long decaying, had begun to fall; the authority not only of school doctrines but of the church had been discarded; while here and there [out of the 'mainstream'] a few devoted experimenters were turning with fresh zeal to the unwithered face of nature. The fruitful thoughts which lay under and gave rise to these scattered efforts of the human mind, were gathered up into unity, and reduced to system in the new philosophy of Bacon.']*

"I knew one that when he wrote a letter he would put that which was most material in the postscript, as if it had been a by matter."

"It has been well said 'the arch-flatterer with whom all the petty flatterers have [communion] with is a man's self.'"

"There is little friendship in the world, and least of all between equals."

"Some books are to be tasted, others to be swallowed, and some few to be chewed and digested."

"Reading makes a full man... writing an exact man."

"The nobelist works and foundations have proceeded from childless men, [who] have sought to express the images of their minds where those of their bodies have failed."

P.S. I honestly intended to write this column without saying a word of my OWN, but: as Nixon used to say, I just want to say this about that:

I'm sure that Bacon never envisioned a time when some men would be childless - not because their bodies had failed, but - because Emperors with no clothes and Judges with no robes failed them and their off-springs in Roe v. Wade (the Latin word for "fetus" means "off-spring," you know).

Bacon said, "It is as natural to die as to be born; and to a little infant, perhaps, the one is as painful as the other."

Dying in a partial-birth abortion, though, is both painful and unnatural, eh?

* The time is ripe for "Crisis #14" by Tom Paine.

Section 4G:
"The Justices' new robes:
Gold-threaded or cold-blooded?"
www.RenewAmerica.us/
columns/dahlgren/031211

"Despotism may govern without faith, but liberty cannot."
- Alexis de Tocqueville

Unborn baby: "Mommy, Mommy - what does abortion have to do with the 'Right to Privacy'?"

Mommy: "Shut up and leave me and your father ALONE!"

Baby (a few years later): "Mommy, Mommy - now that I survived the abortion, can you tell me what the Supreme Court has against Free Speech?"

Mommy: "Shut up and leave me and your stepfather ALONE! And stop calling me Mommy!"

"Yes, your honor."

"Sometimes you don't know if you're Caesar about to cross the Rubicon or Captain Queeg cutting your own tow line."
- Justice Anthony Kennedy (1992)

DECEMBER 11, 2003 will go down as a Day of Infamy in the history of our Republic. Five-to-four, the Supreme Court sold itself out. They confused impudence with jurisprudence. Which part of "Congress shall make no law restricting free speech" do they not understand? Even the ACLU may be confused. Not since the Gag Rules of 1835-1844 have all three branches of our Federal government gone on record as gung-ho against Freedom of Speech. What happened to the "chilling effect" our leftist friends were decrying when CBS scuttled "The Reagans" miniseries (without any government involvement, I might add)?

The Truth About
"Campaign Finance Reform"
(Or The "Incumbent Protection Act"):

The reality is, CBS and ABC, etc., will be able to use "poetic license" and "literary creativity" in the news within 60 days of a general election, and the groups they attack, such as right-to-life groups and the NRA, will not be allowed by law to respond! The SCOTUS, which has ruled that virtual child porn and cable pornography is speech "protected by the Constitution" now says that a group that uses soft money to mention an incumbent's name in a TV ad within 60 days of the election will be classified as a "criminal" group. What more could be "chilling"?

Even eternally optimistic conservative commentators are shocked. I'm not. Neither eternally optimistic nor shocked! It's hard to be an optimist when perhaps 95% of our population didn't even notice this happen, let alone understand the ramifications. Now that the NRL and the NRA have, essentially, been silenced in elections, it's only a matter of time before Big Brother tries to silence or control the very media that supported this "reform"!

Here's an excerpt from a daily reading I do:

> Years ago, an ambassador from another country came to Sparta, a city which, unlike most others in Greece at that time, had no walls. "The city is very fine," he said, "but where are your walls?"
> He was taken outside the city to see the Spartan army lined up all around it... "These are the walls of Sparta," said the guide.
> In a truer sense than that... the men and women and children of a nation are its defense, "the living stones" in its wall. -Today With God (December 11th)

This wall, the true "wall of separation" protecting the churches from the government – the power of the people under the Constitution - is being broken down "chink by chink," exposing us to greater dangers than either Terrorism or the measures created to combat it. Our Founding Fathers cited Life, Liberty, and the Pursuit of Happiness as a sort of tripod of the Union, but with Life and Free Speech no longer sacred, how can the Union stand on one leg? "Happiness" so based and so pursued will soon evaporate from the earth, if America is "the last best hope." Even "chink" is now a "forbidden word."

On the Jefferson Memorial are chiseled these words: "The God who gave us life, gave us liberty at the same time." There are religious words all over the Washington Monument. And on the facade of the Federal court house in Sioux City, Iowa, the engraved words say: "Mercy and justice are met together" (a quote from the Psalms), but the Federal courts keep chipping away at Freedom of Religion and Freedom of Speech. If they succeed, these vain people will have to unchisel publicly-visible words all over this "almost chosen country" (Lincoln's words).

Guides at the United States Supreme Court building tell visitors that the carving of Moses and the 10 Commandments is really about the Bill of Rights (and some French philosopher maybe?). Guides at Monticello tell visitors that Jefferson fathered several children by a slave (when nothing of the sort has been proven), and the Bible was removed from the historic church at Jamestown, Virginia (for fear of what?).

Jefferson would be dumbfounded by today's anti-Jeffersonian "Judges"! His personally written epitaph says: "Author of the Declaration of Independence and the Statute of Virginia for Religious Freedom - and Father of the University of Virginia." I wonder if William Jefferson Blythe Clinton would be able to cite his three most exciting achievements without mentioning "President of the United States," but anyway:

In the said statute for Religious Freedom in Virginia, it says: "We the General Assembly of Virginia do enact that no man shall be compelled to frequent or support any religious worship, place, or ministry whatsoever, nor shall be enforced, restrained, molested, or burthened in his body or goods, or shall otherwise suffer, on account of his religious opinions or belief; but that all men shall be free to profess, and by argument to maintain, their opinions in matters of religion, and that the same in no wise diminish, enlarge, or affect their civil capacities."

And yet, two judges in the southern "circus" said that Judge Moore had to recant and forever hold his peace, essentially because "we must not mention the Name of the Lord," as Amos said. We're talking serious threats to state and local governments here on account of a "civil liberties" union and the "freedom from religion" movement.

In his first inaugural address, Jefferson expressed "support of the State governments in all their rights as the most competent administra[tors] for our domestic concerns and the surest bulwarks against anti republican tendencies," and he closed the address with these words:

> And may that Infinite Power which rules the destinies of the universe lead our councils to what is best, and give them favorable issue for your peace and prosperity.

In "Notes on the State of Virginia" (the only full-length book he ever wrote), Jefferson asked two "dumb questions":

> 1)"Can the liberties of a nation be thought secure when we have removed their only firm basis, a conviction in the minds of the people that these liberties are... the gift of God?" [and]
>
> 2) "THAT THEY ARE NOT TO BE VIOLATED BUT WITH HIS WRATH?"

Thus we have come full circle here. Campaign "reform" is linked to all the other "hot" issues being glamorized by Federal courts and the increasingly secular Supreme Court, plus the Massachusetts supreme court, among others (and the media). We have met the enemy and they are within!

"Massey-Harris 101"

P.S. More people are killed every day than died on September 11, 2001. I'm talking about the most helpless and innocent people - UNBORN BABIES.

> There are a number of us who creep
> Into the world, to eat and sleep,
> And know no reason why we're born
> Save only to consume the corn,
> Devour the cattle, flock, and fish,
> And leave behind an empty dish.
>
> — "God's Minute" (September 11th)

Thomas Paine, where are you? It's time for "Crisis #14."

Conclusion:

The solution must be "of the Spirit."

— General Douglas MacArthur

A) [To begin the concluding remarks of this book, I lead off with my most unusual column.]

"Why Did The English-speaking Peoples Capitalize The Word I?"
Www.renewamerica.us/columns/dahlgren/050112

"I AM THAT I AM."

— God (to Moses, 1492 BC?)

"I am, said I, to no one there."

— Neil Diamond

"I" equates with the "INDIVIDUAL." No ethnic group on earth has done more in times past for the freedom of the individual, and to fight oppression, than the English-speaking peoples, with a little help from the Hebrew-speaking people. Coincidence? "I think not," said I, to no one there.

The German word for "I" is "ich." The Dutch word is "ik." The Greek is "ego." French is "je." Russians say "ja." The Swedes, "jag." The Danes, "jeg." I think the Spanish word is ja, but they all have one thing in common: their personal pronoun starts with the lower case. The English capitalize the word "I" - and I think that that says a lot about the reasons why the American Revolution was so different from all the others the world has ever seen! At the tender age of 33, Jefferson wrote:

"When in the Course of human events, it becomes necessary for one people to dissolve the political bands which have connected them with another, and to assume among the powers of the earth, the separate and equal station to which the Laws of Nature and of Nature's God entitle them, a decent respect to the opinions of mankind requires that they should declare the causes which impel them to the separation.

> "We hold these truths to be self-evident, that all men are created equal, that they are endowed by their Creator with certain unalienable Rights, that among these are Life, Liberty, and the Pursuit of Happiness… "

We are "one people" (plural), but we are first of all individuals: America is not "a glorious mosaic" or a homogenized "collective"; nor is America a little Village. America is a great city shining on the side of a hill (or it used to be).

Jefferson capitalized such words as Laws of Nature, and "Life" - just as the King James Bible capitalized "I AM THAT I AM" - for a reason!

In "21st Century Academia," Jefferson's writing would probably get a D-minus or an F for his excessive use of capital letters. Furthermore, the educrats would try to tell you that he stole his ideas mostly from French

Rationalism, not from religion, even though he read the Bible in four languages, and had actually heard of the Magna Carta (1215 A.D.).

President Reagan said, "The Founding Fathers believed that faith in God was key to our becoming a great nation." Never forget:

The American and French Revolutions were totally different, from conception to "execution," and the differences in the results couldn't be more stark! The American Revolution was founded on positive thinking and faith, while the French Revolution was not only "secular" but viciously anti-religion, and based on vengeance. Ironically, Tocqueville said:

> "The Frenchman constantly raises his eyes above him with anxiety. The Englishman lowers his beneath him with satisfaction."

> America, thou half-brother of the world;
> With something good and bad of every land.
> - Philip James Bailey (1816-1902)

> "God had sifted three kingdoms to find the wheat for this planting."
> - Henry Wadsworth Longfellow (1807-1882), The Courtship of Miles Standish

> "I believe that God in shedding His grace on this country has always in this divine scheme of things kept an eye on our land and guided it as a promised land."
> - Ronald Reagan (1952)

People who come here from messed-up parts of the world including France tend to understand the meaning of "certain unalienable Rights" better than "native-born" Americans. In his morning update [01/11/05], Rush Limbaugh told about a Kuwaiti student who came here to study at a college in Cali-forn-ya:

In one class, the assignment for his final paper was titled: "America was not founded by the people, but by wealthy elitists." The Kuwaiti argued the opposite premise, and he told how grateful he was to America for saving his country from Saddam Hussein (who had killed some of his relatives).

"Professor Woolcock" flunked him and told him that he needed "psychological help"! He especially criticized the student for implying that America is "God's gift to the world!" This is SO typical (sending your precious sons and daughters into the LaLa Land of Academia is like sending them down a rabbit hole into a parallel universe, a nightmare of Satanic proportions.

May God have mercy on this professor - and on US for paying the salaries of such professors! I would advise them to "challenge their most cherished assumptions."

As I said, President Reagan's farewell to the United Nations referred to Washington's Farewell address - how the case for "inalienable rights" and "the notion of conscience above compulsion" can only be made in the context of a Higher Law. That was no "assumption" on the part of Washington or Ronald Reagan. My minister once said that there is no greater curse than to be outside of God's government. He was right.

> "May we think of freedom, not as the right to do as we please, but as the opportunity to do what is right."
>
> - Peter Marshall, Jr.

As usual, that's a great paradox that the liberals can't handle. We have enjoyed unprecedented Freedom to honor that "Higher Law" by the way we live our lives (without persecution). It's time to make our blessings count and not just to count our money. America has been good to us, but paradoxically, equality of opportunity never was intended to mean "equality of outcome" (that's neither a logical nor desirable goal). Ironically, though, America's Freedom coupled with a respect for the Laws of Nature and "Nature's God" gives the individual his best chance of achieving success. The reason we look "backwards" is in order to get a better view into the future – and to put the present in context. Reagan said that "status quo is Latin for the mess we're in."

America without a Reagan is like the Packers without a Bret Favre. When Bret retired this year, he held a press conference and quoted something his wife Deanna had said: "You get more light through the windshield than from the rear view mirror."

Yes, objects in the rear view mirror "may appear closer than they are" - and maybe our Founders appear a bit "larger" than they were, but that's because they "cast long shadows." And we can only ignore their words of warning at our own risk! President Reagan said:

> "The ultimate determinant in the struggle now going on for the world will not be bombs and rockets but a test of wills and ideas - a trial of spiritual resolve."

P.S. For years and years I've been trying to talk people into reading Abraham Lincoln's Cooper Institute Address - without success – but there's a website where you can go to read it, because RIGHT MAKES MIGHT - http://showcase.netins.net/web/creative/lincoln/speeches/cooper.htm

The occasion occurred during what amounted to the "primary campaign" of 1860. Lincoln was still an unannounced candidate, and it was certainly not a political "pep rally." Those were serious times, and what he had to say was serious stuff.

> "In October 1859 Abraham Lincoln accepted an invitation to lecture at Henry Ward Beecher's church in Brooklyn, New York, and chose a political topic which required months of painstaking research. His law partner William Herndon observed, 'No former effort in the line of speech-making had cost Lincoln so much time and thought as this one'...
> "The carefully crafted speech examined the views of the 39 signers of the Constitution. Lincoln noted that at least 21 of them

– a majority – believed Congress should control slavery in the territories, not allow it to expand. Thus, the Republican stance of the time was not revolutionary, but similar to the Founding Fathers, and should not alarm Southerners (radicals had threatened to secede if a Republican was elected President).

"When Lincoln arrived in New York, the Young Men's Republican Union had assumed sponsorship of the speech and moved its location to the Cooper Institute... Lincoln, as an unannounced presidential aspirant, attracted a capacity crowd of 1,500 curious New Yorkers.

"An eyewitness that evening was disappointed when Lincoln rose to speak [because] he was so tall, ungainly, and awkward... However, once Lincoln warmed up, 'his face lighted up as with an inward fire,' the whole man was transfigured. I forgot his clothes, his personal appearance, and his individual peculiarities. Presently, forgetting myself, I was on my feet like the rest, yelling like a wild Indian, cheering this wonderful man.'

"Herndon, who knew the speech but was not present, said it was 'devoid of all rhetorical imagry.' Rather, 'it was constructed with a view to accuracy of statement, simplicity of language, and unity of thought. In some respects like a lawyer's brief, it was logical, temperate in tone, powerful – irresistibly driving home to men's reasons and their souls'...

"Said a New York writer, 'No man ever before made such an impression on his first appeal to a New York audience.' After being printed by New York newspapers, the speech was widely circulated as campaign literature."

NOW THAT WAS A "CAMPAIGN SPEECH"! It accounts for 15 pages of fine print in the biography by Henry J. Raymond, the editor of the New York Times. My copy of the book was given to me when it was only 99 years old; now it is almost 143 years. It is 813 pages long, but came off the presses within a few months of Lincoln's assassination (long before "instant publishing"). One thing for sure, people were more literate 143 years ago. Average citizens actually read the whole speech, though I can't even get our leaders to read it today. And as Raymond said:

"Not the people of his own country alone, but all the world, will study with interest the life and public acts of one whose work was at once so great and so successful." Here's just one juicy tidbit from that speech on a Tuesday evening in New York City, February 27, 1860:

"But you say you are conservative – eminently conservative – while we are revolutionary, destructive, or something of the sort. What is conservatism? Is it not adherence to the old and tried, against a new and untried? We stick to, contend for, the identical old policy on the point in controversy which was adopted by 'our fathers who framed the Government under which we live;' while you with one accord reject, and scout, and spit upon that old policy, and insist upon substituting something new…

"Let us be diverted by none of those sophistical contrivances wherewith we are so industriously plied and belabored – contrivances such as groping for some middle ground between the right and the wrong, vain as the search for a man who should be neither a living man nor a dead man – such as a policy of 'don't care' on a question about which all true men do care – such as Union appeals beseeching true Union men to yield to Disunionists, reversing the divine rule, and calling, not the sinners, but the righteous to repentance – such as invocations to Washington, imploring men to unsay what Washington said, and undo what Washington did.

"Neither let us be slandered from our duty by false accusations against us, nor frightened from it by menaces of destruction to the Government nor of dungeons to ourselves.

"LET US HAVE FAITH THAT RIGHT MAKES MIGHT, AND IN THAT FAITH LET US, TO THE END, DARE TO DO OUR DUTY AS WE UNDERSTAND IT." [caps from the original]

How many pages this book will have, I don't know, but I apologize not for the wordiness. The only thing I apologize for is if I have ever used the term "my book." This isn't MY book - it's Jefferson's, Adams' and Washington's. It's Tocqueville's and Orwell's; Bacon's, Burke's, and Lincoln's - not to mention Isaiah, Jeremiah, or Ezekiel. It was even inspired in part by Bret Favre, who - after an unbelievable game in Oakland right after his father died – said:

"Maybe it's time we started believing in Something."

"The solution must be of the Spirit."

B) [Here's the second half of the Conclusion.]

"THE IMPLICATIONS OF MONOTHEISM:
Does God bless ungrateful nations?"
www.RenewAmerica.us/
columns/dahlgren/071121

"How shall I pardon them for this? Thy children have forsaken me, and sworn by those who are no gods; when I had fed them to the full, they committed adultery."

- Jeremiah

"A God all mercy is a God unjust."

- Edward Young (1807-1889)

MOST AMERICANS CLAIM TO BELIEVE IN GOD. A more important "poll" question would be: "Does God still believe in US?"

We have been standing by as a people and allowing Christianity to be forced back into the closet while simultaneously watching abominations be brought out onto the streets of our once-gleaming alabaster cities. America didn't fall. We were pushed! We were pushed by liberal God-bashers.

The book "The Religion of Abraham Lincoln" says:

"The prophetic note of a God of mercy Who punishes the sins of men in the judgments of history with a view to reformation would become a dominant theme in [Lincoln's] later religious utterances, especially in his presidential proclamations.

"Here Lincoln saw much more clearly than most of the parsons of his day that there is an unbiblical preaching of pardon of sin that, by extricating the individual man from his historical and social setting, gives him illusions about punishment in this world and the next.

"Lincoln understood the gospel to mean the salvation of men in both a this-worldly and a next-worldly framework. Many ministers had reduced Christianity to a message of escape for individuals in the NEXT world." [excuse my emphasis] The author, William Wolf says:

"Isaac Cogdal, who had known Lincoln from the time of the New Salem period, recalled a discussion on religion in Lincoln's office in 1859; Herndon was in the office at the time. Lincoln expressed himself in about these words:

"He did not nor could not believe in the endless punishment of any one of the human race. He understood punishment was parental in its object, aim, and design, and intended for the good of the offender; hence it must cease when justice is satisfied.

"He added this remark, that punishment being 'a provision of the gospel system,' he was not sure but the world would be better off if a little more punishment was preached by our ministers and NOT SO MUCH pardon of sin. This last comment has all the earmarks of an authentic Lincoln utterance." [my emphasis]

By the way, 20 out of 23 ministers in Springfield, Illinois voted against Lincoln in 1860 when he ran for President. He never joined a church and got his "religion" straight out of the Bible from which he learned how to read. When I saw that Bible at his birthplace, I was moved to tears, because our leaders today are "like day-flies warming themselves in the autumnal sunshine without an inkling of the fact that the winter is coming."

P.S. Not to make this entirely into a Jeremiad, but Jeremiah mentions adultery, and I just want to say this about that: Dirty movies and

TV programs are preceded by warnings such as "Adult content" or "For mature audiences." There's an implication there that adultery and fornication are fine if you're an "adult" and "mature." In actuality, John Ayto says:

> "Neither adultery nor the related adulterate have any connection with 'adult.' Both came from the Latin verb adulterare (debauch, corrupt) - with the notion of pollution from some outside source."

That ought to be enough said without further explanation, but one of the problems of dumbed-down education is that most people think that "adultery" can only be committed by a married person, that it's okay for a "single" person. This is a lie that's not even being disputed very much by the graduates of our seminaries (which a wise man used to refer to as "cemeteries" - where the teachers bury the Truth).

On the morning I finalized this section, the temperature outside was about 10 below zero on the 8th of March. Believe it when we tell you that the "Earth" has bigger problems to worry about than footnotes, "carbon foot prints," or "climate change"! Our actual problems are a lot deeper than the mere material and it's a big mistake to ascribe merely physical causes to such problems. It is even more futile to look for mere physical solutions (the Pharaoh of Egypt made that mistake - and look what happened there)! As Kipling said:

> God of our fathers, known of old,
> Lord of our far-flung battle-line,
> Beneath whose awful Hand we hold
> Dominion over palm and pine -
> Lord God of Hosts, be with us yet,
> Lest we forget – lest we forget!...
> For the sin ye do two-by-two, ye must pay for one by one!

More than you can even "imagine," this explains much of the status quo - "the mess we're in."

PPS: I divided the main body of this book into four sections for a reason.

"We have all heard that a million monkeys banging on a million [keyboards] would eventually reproduce the entire works of Shakespeare. Now, thanks to the Internet, we know this is not true."

- Robert Silensky, U. of California
[via DoesGodExist]

GOD'S LOWLY WRITERS HAVE NEVER BEEN SHY ABOUT CALLING A SPADE A SPADE. It appears today that all the people in society can be described as being members of one of the four suits in a deck of cards.

THE SPADES represent people in the practical professions that make society "work," who spend most of their time providing basic needs for themselves and their families. They are the worker bees who leave the "details" to others (and seldom even wonder what's trump).

THE HEARTS, in general, represent all the over-emotional people who assume that the "basic goodness of man" will always be always prevail (many of these people are in education or psychology).

THE DIAMONDS represent the people who wield the pen, some for good and some for evil. Their suit seldom seems to be drawn as trump, but at a few crossroads in human history, it has happened! Think of Tom Paine's, Winston Churchill's, and Ronald Reagan's pens.

THE CLUBS represent the real powers-that-be, including the sword and raw judicial power. Those who over-specialize in the field of power assume that, by reason of their positions, they must be the brightest cards in the deck. But what is really trump right now?

Our Founders put trump in the hands of the Spades, but trump has been essentially stolen from them by the Hearts and Clubs, and the Spades are mostly sleeping through the game (once every four years they wake up and toss a random card into the ballot box). Trump is now usually Clubs or Hearts, but as Bacon said (again):

"There be some who can pack the cards and yet cannot play well."

The bottom line is that the elitists in neither education nor government have been playing well, despite their power. Is it too much to hope, for a change, that trump will finally go to the Diamonds - the New Media and independent thinkers (as in "the pen is mightier than the sword")? I certainly HOPE so, "for a change," and that's why I wrote A Letter to Generation X, Y, and Z, "Massey-Harris 101."

"The solution must be of the Spirit."

- Epilogue -
"Take heed that no man deceive you."

A) [This is one of my favorite columns.]

"Even the seminaries are being driven into the ground" www.RenewAmerica.us/columns/dahlgren/071029

> "Going to church doesn't make you a Christian any more than going to a garage makes you a mechanic."
>
> - author "Unknown"

I CAN NOW SAY THAT I'VE BEEN TO THE UNIVERSITY OF CHICAGO LAW SCHOOL. I made a wrong turn down a dead end street, and had to make a U-turn there. I was in the neighborhood last summer to visit the Oriental Institute, and what a neighborhood it is!

The Chicago Theological Seminary is across the street from this famous Middle Eastern museum. It is surrounded by churches of staggering proportions. They are evidently connected with the "Divinity" schools at the Univ. of Chicago. Some of these churches have bell towers almost ten stories high. It seemed like standing in Europe somewhere looking up at thousand-year-old steeples.

But unfortunately, the Church of the Living God is not a building. The cathedrals may still be sound, but not all the teaching heads at the seminaries are! I felt a cold Halloween shiver as I stood outside the Chicago Theological Seminary last summer.

The politics of religious intellectualism:

A funny story: One time in Escanaba checking out of a department store, I saw the man ahead of me starting to leave without his change, and the clerk reminded him about it. "Thanks," said the old man. "I'll put this in the collection plate next Sunday for their legal defense fund."

A warning: This column may contain certain insensitive excerpts. And these days, "sensitivity" buries the Truth every time in political circles - even in the politics of "theological cemeteries."

An editorial: Under the headline "Sacrificing truth for sensitivity," Madison's Wisconsin State Journal (over 16 years ago, 1/31/92) put its finger on today's number one problem: Truth can be "insensitive," and therefore "must" be silenced (I'm being sarcastic). The editorial said:

> "Anyone who doubts the pervasiveness of political correctness at UW-Madison need look no further than the two campus newspapers. Both have carried items in the past week that prove the role of the press in a free society escapes those students willing to sacrifice truth on the altar of sensitivity.
> "The Badger Herald reported last week that a student member of the Gay and Lesbian Issues Committee was peeved about press coverage of the committee's report. 'By no means is the press covering it the way we want,' the student whined. Well, excuuuuuse us, but we must have cut class the day the journalism instructor said reporters are supposed to ask subjects how they 'want' the news covered."

"You can fool all the people some of the time, and some of the people all the time, but you can not fool all the people all of the time." - Abe Lincoln [September 8, 1858, at Clinton, Illinois]

Now if I say "the Catholics' problem," or "the Episcopal problem," and you understand what I mean, it's obvious to you that our churches in America have a PROBLEM. And if the churches have a "problem," America has a BIG problem!

Remember: The First Amendment not only gives us Freedom of Speech and Freedom of Religion, but this includes Freedom of Speech about Religion, whether people want to hear the Truth or not. The most insidious movement to suppress the Truth is starting to come from within religion itself. If the Islamo-terrorists are patient, we could be destroyed from within by our own churches.

[Since I wrote that paragraph, the Archbishop of Canterbury has stated that England should allow sharia law for Muslims. This is the same guy who says that Christians don't have to believe in the resurrection of Christ or the virgin birth, etc. Rush Limbaugh says, "Start your own religion then, but don't call it Christian."]

Christ predicted that we would be hated by "all nations" for His name's sake (which means Christians and Christian nations would be hated by the U.N., etc.). The church my parents attended didn't actually quote Jesus too often on such "insensitive" subjects, but somehow I was always aware of that prophecy. Not only is persecution increasing around the world, but pressure is being applied on us to roll over and abandon "divisive" issues. This would require us to essentially ignore the Bible in its entirety - because parts of it are insensitive. This tedious process began ages ago, and it picked up speed in the 60s. In November 1962, Decision magazine published an article by Richard Nixon entitled "A Nation's Faith in God." This was about the time of the Cuban missile crisis, and he said:

> "During the years that I spent in Washington, I had the privilege of hearing some of the greatest religious leaders of our generation. Invariably, I received help and inspiration from the messages they

Curtis Dahlgren

brought. But if I might dare to venture a comment, I think that some of our voices in the pulpit today tend to speak too much about religion in the abstract, rather than in the personal, simple terms which I heard in my earlier years.

"More preaching from the Bible, rather than just about the Bible, is what America needs... The American people will not fail if they are summoned to their ultimate commitments and duties, and are recalled to the faith of their fathers.

"Way down inside they know that the fads and fancies and false values of the passing scene count for nothing... But theirs is a faith that ultimately goes back to the fundamental truths of the Bible. In the face of the challenge, I for one look with fresh interest in the days ahead to learning what the Bible has to say to our time." [my emphasis]

That was then. It becomes increasingly difficult to be an optimist when even the seminaries revolt against "the faith of our fathers." In the Sept-Oct 2007 issue of Does God Exist, Joel Stephen Williams speaks about such cultural/religious phenomena:

"The trend is more obvious in the large cities or near major university campuses, because that is where immigrants have usually gathered. People of Anglo-Saxon heritage are converting to non-Christian religions, even though their numbers are quite small. American culture is now very pluralistic.

"Many Christian values and assumptions are no longer considered basic values or assumptions. Not only are Judeo-Christian values no longer taken for granted, there is a widespread effort to diminish those same values, even to silence them and remove them from the public square. As Ravi Zacharias, a Brahman Hindu born in India who converted to Christianity, declared:

Philosophically, you can believe anything, so long as you do not claim it to be true. Morally, you can practice anything, so long as you do not claim that it is a 'better' way. Religiously, you can hold to anything, so long as you do not bring Jesus Christ into it. If a spiritual idea is eastern, it is granted critical immunity; if western, it is thoroughly criticized. Thus, a journalist can walk into a church and mock its carryings on, but he or she dare not do the same if the ceremony is from the eastern fold. Such is the mood at the end of the twentieth century.

[Jesus Among Other Gods: The Absolute Claims of the Christian Message," Word Pub.]

> "The purpose of this brief study is to outline some of the problems a Christian faces in trying to live a life of faith in a pluralistic society and to point in the direction of an appropriate Christian response to non-Christian beliefs."

P.S. The Beatles sang about a "world without religion" and then IMAGINED that "there will be an 'answer.'" You can't have it both ways. The world will go on reaping what it sows whether we have a world with or without religion. That's the Law of Nature. As Tocqueville said, "When America ceases to be good, America will cease to be great." The same goes for England and France, if it's not too late.

As believers, we need to get "mad" and tell preachers we're not going to take it anymore when they preach "about" the Bible instead of FROM the Bible (even as the public educators teach "about" the Founding Fathers instead of words FROM the Founders). Evangelism is about repentance, not just "recruitment" or "enlistment" of new members. The Truth shall make you Free.

If there is indeed going to be an "ANSWER," the solution must be "of the Spirit.

America: Look Up, Phone Home, And Bless God!

B) [This may not be my most entertaining column, but it's probably the most important one.]

"Think-giving Day: Count your blessings, but make your blessings count!"
www.RenewAmerica.us/
columns/dahlgren/031120

Curtis Dahlgren

"The preacher sought to find out acceptable words, even words of truth. The words of the wise are like cattle prods... for God shall bring every work into judgment."

- Solomon

FREEDOM AND PROSPERITY HAVE BEEN PROVEN TO GO TOGETHER, BUT- some people compound their ingratitude with counter-productive, self-destructive attitudes that could destroy both their freedom and their means of physical survival. While some believe that there is no right or wrong at all, some believe that there is a right and a wrong about almost every subject except economics.

"Opportunities always look bigger going than coming," someone said. The book in your hands has given you a rare window of opportunity to look both into the rear view mirror and into the future. Whether you choose to look through rose-colored glasses, a heavily-tinted windshield, or through the eye-glasses of realistic expectations is entirely up to you. Your "salvation" is none of my business, but I have over 65 years invested in this country, and I will not stand by silently and watch it circle the drain (whether you "can hear me now," or not).

"As writers become more numerous, it is natural for readers to become more indolent."

- Oliver Goldsmith (1728-1774)

In "Leadership," James McGregor Burns says that President Reagan was a "transformational" leader - one who doesn't make "deals" but who changes minds: "His conviction shone through."

His "convictions" weren't confined to foreign policy and economics only. Ronald Reagan was a complete leader who not only saw his task as one of bringing down double-digit inflation and the Communists, but also bucking up the churches of the land. Too many Christians have the attitude of people in Central Park who just watch a mugging without doing anything about it - the don't want to get "involved," but in 1983, he told the National Association of Evangelicals:

> "I urge you to beware the temptation of pride - the temptation of blithely declaring yourselves above it all and label both sides equally at fault, to ignore the facts of history and... thereby remove yourself from the struggle between right and wrong and good and evil."

The same year, he wrote an essay on abortion and infanticide that was published as a little 96-page book by Thomas Nelson in 1984 ("Abortion and the Conscience of the Nation"). Here's just a sample:

> "Our nation-wide policy of abortion-on-demand through all nine months of pregnancy was neither voted for by our people nor enacted by our legislatures - not a single state had such unrestricted abortion before the Supreme Court decreed it to be national policy...
>
> "Make no mistake, abortion-on-demand is not a right granted by the Constitution. No serious scholar, including one disposed to agree with the Court's result, has argued that the framers of the Constitution intended to create such a right. Shortly after the Roe v. Wade decision, Professor John Hart Ely, now Dean of Stanford law school, wrote that the opinion 'is not constitutional law and gives almost no sense of an obligation to try to be.'"

As for those who say they don't know when life begins, but nevertheless kill the unborn baby, Reagan said, "If you don't know whether a body is alive or dead, you would never bury it."

In the introduction to the book, Malcolm Muggeridge wrote, "On such vital moral issues as abortion, politicians tend to sit on the fence, hoping to pick up a few votes from both sides. Your President Reagan is the only example I've come across in half a century of knockabout journalism of a political leader ready to stand up without any reservations for the sanctity of life rather than for what passes for being the quality of life."

Young women today are becoming more pro-life, so Reagan's efforts weren't wasted, but too many people have just surrendered to the old public relations idea of "consensus." They have been hustled to believe that "most people want" abortion-on-demand. And too many church leaders tell their members not to "get involved." Reagan said:

> "The future of our country, the direction that we go as a people, whether we move ahead to meet the challenges of the future or slide back into the irresponsible policies of the past, will be determined by those who get involved." [March 6, 1984]

In the Intro to that little book, J.P. McFadden wrote also: "After the Nazi Holocaust, it was charged that those who knew what was happening (great men among them) failed to halt the slaughter… Nothing in history is inevitable; men choose, and we Americans can choose to halt the slaughter of our own innocents. If we do not, history will record… that we were not failed by our great men, that our own president called upon us to make the choice."

Germany and the whole European continent were significantly failed by liberal clergymen, too. "There is an answer" to church leaders who tell you, "Don't get involved" - a very unambiguous scripture that I have never heard expounded in over 65 years of "going to church." Peter said:

> ". . For so is the will of God, that with well doing you may put to silence the ignorance of foolish men; as FREE, and not using your Freedom for a cloak of maliciousness, but as 'bondslaves' of God."
>
> [I Peter 2:15-16]

The Revised Standard Version says, ". . For it is God's will that by doing right you should put to silence the ignorance of foolish men. Live as free men, yet without using your freedom as a pretext for evil, but live as servants of God." That is a part of what is probably Peter's longest sentence (but what is so hard to understand?). Would it be clearer or "plainer" if I restated it the other way around?:

"Use your Freedom to put to silence the ignorance of foolish men."

There's an example of "teaching from the Bible rather than about the Bible." That's my favorite passage in the Bible, but do you "get it" yet? Let me be "perfectly clear":

The context of these two verses talks about civic leaders, so the subject there is "civil liberties," not some ethereal, spiritualized "freedom." Peter says, "Honor all men," too. The Greek word inspired there means to "value" all men (including our enemies, for whom we pray). "Value all men" gets back to the concept of the capital "I" in the English language. Every human being has a God-given value (including the humans not quite born yet)!

Peter wasn't so stupid as to encourage the people of Judea to rise up against the Roman army, but the book of I Peter was written to Christian converts in Asia Minor, the same area where Paul spoke to the philosophers on Mars' Hill in Athens. I hate to have to point out the blatantly obvious, but those people in Asia Minor had more Freedom of Thought and Speech than the people who were more under the Roman thumb (as in the Holy Land). So, you don't have to search for an "excuse" to get involved. It's a commanded requirement of us (even though we don't have to resort to intimidation the way Academia does). Facts are very stubborn things, and a good simple answer will "silence" enemies of the Truth.

By the way, what about the right to vote? What more peaceful way could there be to "put to silence" the ignorance of foolish men? I know some people who think that voting is a "sin" though, because their "citizenship" is in the Kingdom of God (they think). When I told an old friend that I was writing a weekly column for RenewAmerica, the first words out of his mouth were, "You haven't gone political, have you?" Well, should any reader of this book try to say that I'm "too political," I'll "come back, kid" you with the following facts:

1) Joseph "got involved" in the government of Egypt, was in essence the Prime Minister, and saved thousands of lives from famine (not to

mention Moses, who got "involved" later - and saved the Israelites from Egypt).

2) Esther was "involved" in the government of a kingdom that reigned "from India to Ethiopia," became the queen of Persia, and saved thousands of Jews from genocide.

3) Nehemiah was "involved" with the government of the king of Persia, was the official wine taster for the king, and helped save the temple rebuilding project in Jerusalem.

4) Daniel was "involved" with the government of Babylon, was made one of three "presidents" over the princes of the land, and wrote some prophecies that could help save millions of people in the future.

5) The prophet Zephaniah was the great-great grandson of King Hezekiah, king of Israel (and was also related to King Josiah), so he was a bit "involved." He made important prophecies for the nation that are still being worked out at the present time (some of the other prophets, too, came from families that were, or had been, "politically" involved).

6) David and Solomon were not only "involved" but they WERE kings, and they wrote major parts of the Hebrew Bible (one of the things Solomon wrote about was the ideal woman's ideal husband: "he is known in the gates and sits among the elders of the land").

7) The apostle Paul was an intellectual who had been "involved" with the Pharisees and the famous school of Gamaliel in Jerusalem, and was sent to save uncounted Gentiles because he could speak their "language" (both the small and "great"), and he witnessed to Caesar himself. And the two witnesses of Revelation are certainly going to be a bit "involved."

I could go on and on, but you have probably gotten the point by now. A "dumb" question: Why would the God of Israel, who put all those men - plus Esther and Deborah - in such positions, suddenly tell His servants not to get "involved" and stop putting them in positions close to power? Enough said?

Pathetically, the spiritual offspring of the Israelites are so poorly educated in history, that 23 percent of British teenagers think that Winston Churchill was a fictitious character, although 58 percent of them believe that Sherlock Holmes was real. In America, most teens can't name the three branches of government, but 59 percent can name the Three Stooges! They've probably never heard of Nehemiah or Zephaniah, and our half-brother Churchill must be spinning in his grave.

Speaking of "memories," Churchill said: "Do not let us speak of darker days; let us rather speak of sterner days… and we must thank God that we have been allowed, each of us according to our stations, to play a part in making these days memorable in the history of our race."

What is your part going to be? Are you just "salt in the wounds?" Do you turn people off? We need "balance" of course, but balance is not in the middle of the road, but somewhere between the middle of the road and the cliff off to the right. The world needs love all right - tough love. Salt can be used as an astringent, and the "salt of the earth" ought to be a sterner, more austere medicine for what ails society than religion is today.

> "I am only one, but I am one. I cannot do everything, but I can do something. What I can do, I should do and, with the help of God, I will do!"
>
> - Everett Hale

As Rudyard Kipling wrote:

> Land of our birth, we pledge to thee
> Our love and toil in the years to be;
> When we are grown and take our place,
> As men and women with our race.
>
> Father in Heaven who lovest all,
> Oh, help Thy children when they call;
> That they may build from age to age
> AN UNDEFILED HERITAGE.

Curtis Dahlgren

"The Salt of the Earth" is sort of "square," but salt is certainly not one-dimensional. This little "square" cube is one of the most versatile of all creations. It makes grapefruit taste sweet and other food salty. It is a purifier and can be used as a gargle or a preservative, and it increases thirst (just as we ought to increase society's thirst for spiritual knowledge). In olden times, when two people reconciled from an "offense," they would put salt on a plate, lick their forefinger, dip it in the salt, and eat it as a sign of friendship. In some cultures, you can still hear the expression, "There is salt between us."

A little boy once said, "Some people use salt to melt ice and some people use salt to make ice cream. Maybe someday we'll find out who's right."

True believers ought to soften hearts and solidify faith, but never mind, for the moment, which branch of religion is "right." There's no need to argue that issue so long as we first agree that faith in general is necessary for a "civilized" world. I write for Alan Keyes' website, and I think he's a Catholic. I think the editor of the website may be a Mormon. I'm neither - and no doubt our writers represent many other denominations - but as Tocqueville once wrote:

> "Though it is very important for man as an individual that his religion should be true, that is not the case for society. Society has nothing to fear or hope from another life; what is most important for it is not that all citizens profess the true religion but that they should profess religion."

Amen to that! We have more Freedom of Religion than any other people on earth, so USE it! America is too young to die. Make your blessings count – especially the greatest blessing of all - Freedom.

What Does "Thanksgiving" Mean?

Why are we Americans so prosperous? Educators tend to give credit to education, while bureaucrats credit social programs; "labor" credits the unions - while MBAs give the credit to business. Some give the glory to FDR or JFK or 401Ks, but no one asks the farmer. Or God.

Abraham Lincoln said that America became a great and prosperous power because God had given us "the richest soil in the most salubrious climes of the earth." Put me down as agreeing with Lincoln! He knew exactly why he was thankful. And I want to tell you something you probably never heard before about the word "thanksgiving":

The English word "thanks" goes back to the prehistoric Germanic thengk. The same root that gave the Germans "denken" - or "think" - gave us thank. Gratitude wasn't even involved in the word "thank" until the 14th century. It evolved from "thought" to "favourable thought" to, finally, "gratitude."

"THOUGHTS" and "THANKS," therefore came to overlap! Gratitude should follow "reason" and "thought" as logically as the dawn follows the darkest hour of the night. Thanksgiving Day isn't an emotional or irrational sentimentality, but the epitome of reason and rationality - a joint effort of the heart and the MIND! Still, just counting your blessings isn't enough. Be sure to make them count!

"Unto whom much is given, much shall be required."

- Luke

"Required"? I realize that it will come as a shock to some people to hear that their Creator ever "requires" anything of us, but as the song says, "There will be an answer." You just heard it!

The solution must be "of the Spirit."

P.S. DO YOU REALIZE THAT TODAY'S "smartest, healthiest, and hippest generation" can't even understand the phrase, "The solution must be of the Spirit, if we are to save the flesh"? That simply does not compute!

Curtis Dahlgren

I was eight years old when General MacArthur was fired for trying too hard to win the Korean War. My family went to Milwaukee to see him in one of his home-coming parades, although I had to go to school that day. He was from Milwaukee and in April 1951 MacArthur addressed a joint session of Congress, and his exact quote was:

> "Military alliances, balances of power, leagues of nations, all in turn failed, leaving the only path to be by way of the crucible of war. The utter destructiveness of war now blocks out this alternative. We have had our last chance. If we will not devise some greater and more equitable system, our Armageddon will be at our door. The problem basically is theological and involves a spiritual recrudescence, an improvement of human character that will synchronize with our almost matchless advances in science, art, literature, and all material and cultural developments of the past two thousand years. It must be of the spirit if we are to save the flesh."
>
> "For behold, the Lord, the Lord of hosts, doth take away... the mighty man and the man of war, the judge and the prophet, the prudent and the ancient, the captain of fifty and the honourable man, the counsellor and the eloquent orator, and I will give children to be their princes, and babes shall rule over them."
>
> - Isaiah

That's not "funny." As Professor "X" wrote in "This Beats Working for a Living":

> "I would seriously question that this is the smartest generation ever. They may have more facts at their disposal [thanks to TV and the Internet]... Yet today's children have the same body chemistry with which to contend - the emotional instability that simultaneously clouds thinking and causes pimples...
>
> "For example, the people of my generation when young cheered at the movies when the cavalry arrived to rout the Indians; today the young cheer the Indians and boo the soldiers... And today's generation is just as guilty of thinking

emotionally rather than rationally... The thoughts of youth may be long, long thoughts, as the poet told us, but all too often they also are full of inconsistencies, ignorance, and downright stupidity."

The Cold War is being replaced by a worldwide Culture "war" and we're going to lose it (if we can't even define our culture, how can we defend it?). The final chosen quotation was written during the Cold War by Dr. Arthur Voobis. It still APPLIES:

"The world is in agony and we are sleeping. It is a beginning of recovery when we feel that before God we all bear some degree of responsibility and guilt for the degradation into which the world has sunk. What the precise degree of guilt of each individual is becomes a matter of only secondary importance...

"[We have to] regain that fundamental attitude which does not understand faith merely as a gift, but as a chance. And this chance must be so seriously understood that in the risk of trial and test it exemplifies its genuineness."

What are you waiting for anyway? Leo Durocher used to say, "Nice guys, finish last." While it's easy to misinterpret that, most old adages have an element of Truth to them. I know I said that was all for the quotations, but just "one more thing." Leo also said:

"You don't save a pitcher for tomorrow. Tomorrow it may rain... How you play the game is for college boys. When you're playing for money, winning is the only thing that matters."

"'In prison, the important thing is to guard your strength and maintain your health.' This was the advice I received from a friend a few days before my arrest, and at first I agreed with it. But as a zek I soon came to understand an important principle: if you want to remain the same free man you were before your arrest, if you don't want to wind up in the ranks of the loyal Soviet citizens – those slaves who don't dare express their opinions, who justify themselves with such simplistic arguments as 'I'm just a little man, nothing depends on me,' 'You can't chop wood with a penknife,' or 'Why beat your head against the wall' – and if you don't want to become a laboratory rat in the hands of the KGB, you must resist!"

- Natan Sharansky in "Fear No Evil"

You will be "tested" on this book later. Knowledge is power, so don't save your best trump cards for "someday." I want y'all to turn off the TV and do some "critical thinking" for a change. As the writers all say, you need to WAKE UP (unless you like leaving your head in the sand). There was an old French song entitled "Ne pas perdre la tete" ("Don't lose your head"), and as Cowper wrote:

> Freedom has a thousand charms to show,
> That slaves, howe'er contented, never know...
> Men deal with life as children in their play,
> Who first misuse, then cast their toys away...

Spring is beginning to spring in the sandy Peninsulas of Michigan. The mourning doves are calling, "The Ides of March, the Ides of March remember!"

The End: March 12, 2008 [the third anniversary of the violent deaths of eight close friends]

- Addendum -
"Back to School: DESSERTS can save your life"

The Top Ten tips for "True Believers" only ("and the next day it snowed"):

> "There are two ways of spreading the light. One is to be the candle, and the other is to be the mirror that reflects the light."
> - Edith Wharton (1862-1937)

IF YOU ARE A "TRUE BELIEVER," you already know that "perilous times" are upon us, so we had better reflect the True light (the light of the One Who said, "Let there be light"). In such perilous times, the "salt of the earth" could come to be viewed as salt in the wounds, unless we reflect the one True Light, so here are some suggestions:

1: Don't let the "cares of this world" get you down; avoid the liberal trap of humorlessness (they have nearly made laughter illegal)!

A) People who take themselves too seriously are an easy target for their enemies; that's what makes Sam Harris and Richard Dawkins such easy targets for us (in a "loving" way of course). Now when the Bible says "Seek first the Kingdom of God," it means exactly that, but we don't usually notice that there was also humor in that passage! During the translation into our native languages, the body language and tone of voice and little winks and nods by original speakers get lost. But by using the imagination, I think that Matthew 6:32 is one of the Bible's more hilarious verses! How so, you ask?

Well, Christ was saying, "Don't fret about eat or drink or clothing," but then He said a funny thing: "For after all these things do the GENTILES seek."

Perhaps there was a "Gentile" in His audience (maybe even a Jew-hating gentile). Maybe this little side comment was a pithy one at the moment - spoken with a wink-and-a-nod that made some of His disciples smile. After all, was Christ not implying that the Gentiles are the ones who are stereotypically preoccupied with "the material"? Yes, in fact, He was!

B) When John the Baptist saw the Pharisees coming to hear him speak, John said, "Who told you snakes to flee from the wrath to come?" The way I take that is, John himself had never used the words "Flee from the wrath to come," but the Pharisees had just assumed, stereotypically, that that's the language he used (and they had come to be amused). John turned the tables on them so fast that they hadn't even arrived yet (and the disciples of John probably had a hard time keeping a straight face when they saw the twinkle in his eye).

Christ said that "of all men," none were greater than John the Baptist, and so - even though he lived in the "wilderness" - he could hold his own in any conversation with anyone anywhere (no doubt). The attitude of "the snakes," though, was that True Believers were uneducated "hicks" who used nothing but "flee from the wrath to come" words. John was able to quote his contemporaries as well as history, so let that be a warning to anyone who looks on "True Believers" today with a sneer or a smirk.

"Massey-Harris 101"

When it comes to being uneducated, "the smeller's the feller," they say, so maybe the elitists need to go "back to school" - which reminds me of a Rodney Dangerfield story. He said that his wife looked at his desk calendar one day and said, "Who's April? And who's MAY?"

God has a sense of humor. Those five words might knock some readers off their chairs, but you might check out a few scriptures in Psalms. 1-

2: Pray about the things the Lord told you to pray about (such as, your enemies!):

A) I wrote a column about that ("The Top Ten things to pray for"), and you could read it here:

www.RenewAmerica.us/columns/dahlgren/051229 [Hint: God never said to "Pray for world peace" (the only exception was, "pray for the peace of Jerusalem").]

B) Never forget Thanksgiving. Two of the better columns on this subject were in my first book, and you can read them for free by going to:

www.RenewAmerica.us/columns/dahlgren/031120 ("Think-giving; what made America great") www.RenewAmerica.us/columns/dahlgren/040120 ("A farmer's State of the Union message")

It really did snow today, on the 13th of March, but I'm thankful for that (even if I had laundry hanging on the line). Anyway, those were the first two tips! The last eight tips follow below.

- -Dedication (to a cause higher than oneself)
- -Enthusiasm (meaning "God-in-us")
- -Spiritual-mindedness
- -Substance-over-symbolism
- -Expectations ("Faith")
- -Responsibility
- -Truthfulness
- -SUCCESS

Those "DESSERTS" can save your life! But each point has its counterpart:

-Self-centeredness
-Thanklessness
-Rationalizations
-Emotionalism-over-substance
-Society (pop culture)
-Satanism
-Envy
-DEFEAT

"Desserts" spelled backwards spells STRESSED. The "seven deadly sins" can give you seven sleepless nights per week! Words mean things, even one such as "deviltry" (or "devilment," as it used to be called in the south).

Thou hast been call'd, O Sleep! the friend of Woe,
But 'tis the happy who have called thee so...

From his brimstone bed, at break of day
A walking the Devil is gone,
To look at his little snug farm of the World,
And see how his stock went on.

- Robert Southey (1774-1843)

"The ides of March are come."

- Caesar

"Ay, Caesar; but not gone."

- Soothsayer

P.S. One final quotation: "This gospel of the Kingdom shall be preached in all the world as a witness to all nations, and then shall come THE END." Oh, and as Columbo used to say, "Just one other thing":

For all sad words of tongue or pen,
The saddest are these: 'It might have been!'

- John Greenleaf Whittier (1807-1892)

PPS: I was writing this section on the anniversary of the funeral of the last friend laid to rest from a shooting in 2005. I was on my way to that meeting place that day for a special "pot luck." It's a long story, and a long journey, but I didn't make it, even though I used to sit in the very chairs where many of the victims sat that day. I want to thank my Ghost Writers in the Sky for saving me to fight another day. This is Their book - and a book for eight close friends lost to "devilment."

… They killed him in his kindness,
In their madness in their blindness,
And they killed him from behind…
He lies in his blood -
The Father in his face…
There is sobbing of the strong,
And a pall upon the land;

- Herman Melville

And diff'ring judgements serve but to declare
That truth lies somewhere, if we knew but where…
Thousands kiss the book's outside who ne'er look within…

God moves in a mysterious way
   His wonders to perform;
He plants His footsteps in the sea,
   And rides upon the storm…
And Satan trembles when he sees
   The weakest saint upon his knees.

- William Cowper (1731-1800)

[Today was the 19th of March, 2008 – the same day Mikhail Gorbachev came out of his "prayer closet" and admitted his faith by praying in public. As Bret Favre says, "Maybe it's time we started believing in Something.")]

PPPS: As Columbo said, "Just one more thing." On March 21st, another foot of snow fell on the old Midwest ("Thanks for nothing, Al Gore."). Snow piles in town are still higher than one's head in the U.P. As William Cowper wrote, it's "Our severest winter, commonly called the spring."

[This final draft was completed on Mother's Day, 2008, and the United States has just suffered our 29th coldest April in about 140 years. I cut down a large tree on May 8th, and believe it or not, there was still ICE inside the tree trunk! If there's a final lesson in there somewhere, it's "don't believe everything you read" - especially about "global warming" - and believe virtually nothing you see in motion pictures.]

But whatever day it is when you read these words, it's a good day to ask yourself a question: "Do you know if you will live again?" If the answer is "I don't know," here's your sign: that's your answer!

Is that good enough for you? I hope that you do not overlook the obvious: WE DO HAVE A CHOICE.

- *Appendix* -

Acknowledgments for the following great resources (and recommended reading):

www.RenewAmerica.us
Encyclopaedia Britannica, 11th edition (1910)
Messages and Papers of the Presidents (through Wilson, by Act of Congress, 1894)
The Life, Public Services and State Papers of Abraham Lincoln, by Raymond (1865)
Christianity and the Constitution, the Faith of Our Founding Fathers, Eidsmoe (Baker Books)
The Christian Life and Character of the Civil Institutions of the United States (1864) -
    American Vision; 3150A Florence Rd.; Powder Springs, GA 30127
The Oxford Dictionary of Quotations, Second Edition (1953); Oxford Univ. Press
The Book of Quotes, by Barbara Rowes (Ballantine, 1979)
Leaves of Gold, 11th edition (An anthology of Prayers, Memorable Phrases, Inspirational Verse
    and Prose from the Best Authors of the Word, Both Ancient and Modern)

Democracy in America by Alexis de Tocqueville (Penguin Books version, 2003)
Letter From a Christian Citizen, by Douglas Wilson
The Dawkins Delusion?; by Alister McGrath and Joanna McGrath
http://theroadtoemmaus.org/RdLb/21PbAr/Apl/FlewTheist.htm
Strong's Exhaustive Concordance of the Bible
The Communist Menace, the Present Chaos and Our Christian Responsibility, Arthur Voobis
Freefall of the American University, by Jim Nelson Black
BRAINWASHED: How Universities Indoctrinate America's Youth, by Ben Shapiro
Fish Out of Water: Surviving and Thriving on a Secular Campus, by Abbey Nye
This Beats Working for a Living, by Professor "X" (Arlington House, 1973)
The Heterodoxy Handbook; How to Survive the PC Campus; David Horowitz and Peter Collier
Liberal Fascism, by Jonah Goldberg
White Guilt, by Shelby Steele
Our Character, Our Future, by Alan Keyes
Masters of the Dream, by Alan Keyes
My Grandfather's Son, by Clarence Thomas
Competition As A Dynamic Process, by John Maurice Clark (Brookings Inst., 1961)
America in 1857; A Nation on the Brink, Kenneth Stampp (Oxford Univ. Press, 1990)
The Religion of Abraham Lincoln, by William J. Wolf (1963)
Abortion and the Conscience of the Nation, by Ronald Reagan (Thos. Nelson, pub.)
Tom Paine; Freedom's Apostle, by Leo Gurko (Thomas Crowell C., 1957)
A Nation of Victims; the Decay of the American Character, Chas. Sykes (St. Martin's)
A Deficit of Decency, by Zell Miller
Dictionary of Word Origins, by John Ayto (Arcade, 1990)
State of Fear, by Michael Crichton
The Politically Incorrect Guide to Global Warming and

Environmentalism, by
    Christopher C. Horner (Regnery Pub., 2007)
Climate Confusion, by Dr. Roy Spencer
Americans No More; the Death of Citizenship, by Georgie Anne Geyer (Atlantic Monthly, 1996)
What Would the Founders Do?; Our Questions, Their Answers; by Richard Brookhiser
What Can a Man Do?, by Milton Mayer
The Fenton Bible; translation by Ferrar Fenton
The Rebirth of America, by the Arthur S. DeMoss Foundation (1986)
Markings, by Dag Hammarskjold
Liberalism is a Mental Disorder, by Michael Savage (Nelson Current, 2005)
How to Talk to a Liberal (If You Must), Ann Coulter, Crown Forum (esp. "Sally Does Monticello")
The Way Things Ought to Be, by Rush Limbaugh (Pocket Books, 1992)
Postmodern Times; A Christian Guide to Contemporary Thought and Culture, by Gene Edward Veith, Jr. (Crossway Books)
Eye to Eye; Facing the Consequences of Dividing Israel, by William Koenig (About Him Pub.; PO Bx 25812, Alexandria, VA 22313)
The Things Trees Know, by Douglas Wood (Adventure Pub.; Cambridge, MN 55008)
The Power of the Positive Woman, by Phyllis Schlafley (Arlington House, 1977)
The Beast on the East River, by Nathan Tabor
Get Off My Honor, by Hans Zeiger
Silent Witness, by Mark Fuhrman
God and Man at Yale, by William F. Buckley, Jr.
Free to Choose, by Milton and Rose Friedman
Aborting America, by Bernard Nathanson, M.D
Life Is For Living, by Betty Carlson
One American Must Die, by Kurt Carlson
The Right to Live: The Right to Die, by C. Everett Koop (Tyndale House, 1976)
[and anything written by Thomas Sowell]

www.reaganranch.org
www.nronline.com
www.patriotpost.us
www.townhall.com
www.WorldNetDaily.com

www.quotationspage.com
www.brainyquotes.com
www.cblpi.org

Further "required reading materials":

NO MORE BULL: America, Please Phone Home, by Curtis Dahlgren (AuthorHouse, 2004)
Martyrdom in Milwaukee, by Thomas M. Geiger (Helenville, WI 53137)
www.RenewAmerica.us/columns/dahlgren/050321 - "Terry, Terry - O Terri"
www.RenewAmerica.us/columns/dahlgren/050112 - "Why do such things have to happen?"
www.RenewAmerica.us/columns/dahlgren/070405 - "April 5, 1964: the end of an era"
www.RenewAmerica.us/columns/dahlgren/040626 - "Remembering Ronald Reagan"
www.RenewAmerica.us/columns/dahlgren/060625 - "The Univ.of Wis. on Darwinism"
www.RenewAmerica.us/columns/dahlgren/070127 - "The Top Ten most un-PC scriptures"
www.RenewAmerica.us/columns/dahlgren/061114 - "The politics of intellectualism"
www.RenewAmerica.us/columns/dahlgren/061027 - "Politics of religious intellectualism"
www.RenewAmerica.us/columns/dahlgren/050427 - "A short course on Edmund Burke"
www.RenewAmerica.us/columns/dahlgren/060830 - "Ashkelon in the Moonlight"
www.RenewAmerica.us/columns/dahlgren/060917 - "The road from Damascus to Liberal"

"Massey-Harris 101"

www.RenewAmerica.us/columns/dahlgren/050305 - "A Tale of Two Writers"
Fear No Evil, by Natan Sharansky (Random House, 1988)
The Autobiography of Herbert W. Armstrong - HWA

1- Oh, just "one more thing" (I suppose every history book deserves at least one footnote): A little boy was looking at the family Bible on the coffee table one day, and his mother asked him what was on his mind. The little boy looks up and says, "Is this really God's book?"

She said, "Yes, it certainly is." And the little boy says:

> "Well, I think that we should give it back to Him, because nobody around here reads it anyway."

Most people today don't even know what a manger is, but there's a reason He was born in a manger. A manger is a feed box, and He is our spiritual food, the Bread of Life, and we are supposed to "feed" on the Word. There was also spiritual symbolism at the end of His earthly pilgrimage. When He rose from the dead, He carefully folded the napkin that had been placed over His face. So?

Accordingly to tradition, when the rich people of that time got up from the table, they would leave the napkin in disarray if they were finished so that the servants would know that they were finished. If they were going to return, they would fold the napkin. Christ isn't finished; He's going to return!

> Judge not the Lord by feeble sense,
>   But trust Him for His grace;
> Behind a frowning providence
>   He hides a smiling face…
> Sometimes a light surprises
>   The Christian while he sings;
> It is the Lord who rises
>   With healing in His wings.
>
>   - William Cowper

He's not smiling YET, though. Milton Mayer said, "St. Thomas said something about God… that comes back to me. He said that getting to know God is like getting to know a country – you have got to live there." Where I live, it was snowing on "Easter Sunday" and a cold wind's still blowing, but anyway folks, it's time to put the little ones to bed and close the covers on this one, because "That's all she wrote."

OR, as Noah said when he closed the door on the ark, IT'S TIME TO PUT HER IN THE WATER.

- The End. [Submitted May 12, 2008]

Made in the USA
Lexington, KY
06 December 2009